TURNING LEARNING RIGHT SIDE UP

TURNING LEARNING RIGHT SIDE UP:

PUTTING EDUCATION BACK ON TRACK

Russell L. Ackoff, Daniel Greenberg

© 2008 by Pearson Education, Inc.
Publishing as Wharton School Publishing
Upper Saddle River, New Jersey 07458

Wharton School Publishing offers excellent discounts on this book when ordered in quantity for bulk purchases or special sales. For more information, please contact U.S. Corporate and Government Sales, 1-800-382-3419, corpsales@pearsontechgroup.com.
For sales outside the U.S., please contact International Sales at international@pearsoned.com.

Printed in the United States of America

First Printing June 2008

ISBN-10 0-13-234649-4
ISBN-13 978-0-13-234649-8

Pearson Education LTD.
Pearson Education Australia PTY, Limited.
Pearson Education Singapore, Pte. Ltd.
Pearson Education North Asia, Ltd.
Pearson Education Canada, Ltd.
Pearson Educatión de Mexico, S.A. de C.V.
Pearson Education—Japan
Pearson Education Malaysia, Pte. Ltd.

Library of Congress Cataloging-in-Publication Data

Ackoff, Russell Lincoln, 1919-

Turning learning right side up : putting education back on track / Russell L. Ackoff and Daniel Greenberg.

p. cm.

Includes bibliographical references.

ISBN-13: 978-0-13-234649-8 (hardback : alk. paper)

ISBN-10: 0-13-234649-4 (hardback : alk. paper) 1. Education—Aims and objectives. 2. Education—Philosophy. I. Greenberg, Daniel A. (Daniel Asher), 1934- II. Title.

LB41.A184 2008

370.1—dc22

2007038247

Vice President, Publisher:
Tim Moore

Associate Publisher and Director of Marketing:
Amy Neidlinger

Wharton Editor:
Yoram (Jerry) Wind

Acquisitions Editor:
Martha Cooley

Editorial Assistant:
Pamela Boland

Operations Manager:
Gina Kanouse

Digital Marketing Manager:
Julie Phifer

Publicity Manager:
Laura Czaja

Assistant Marketing Manager:
Megan Colvin

Cover Designer:
Alan Clements

Managing Editor:
Kristy Hart

Copy Editor:
Keith Cline

Proofreader:
San Dee Phillips

Senior Indexer:
Cheryl Lenser

Senior Compositor:
Gloria Schurick

Manufacturing Buyer:
Dan Uhrig

To the children at Sudbury Valley School

Contents

About the Authors

Russell L. Ackoff is the Anheuser-Busch Professor Emeritus of Management Science, the Wharton School, and a Distinguished Affiliated Faculty member, Center for Organizational Dynamics, both at the University of Pennsylvania. He also holds a visiting chair in the Centre for Systems Studies at the University of Hull in the United Kingdom. He has served as a visiting professor at the National Autonomous University of Mexico, the University of Birmingham (U.K.), Lisbon University, and Washington University (St. Louis). He received a Bachelor of Architecture in 1941 and a Ph.D. in philosophy of science (1947) from the University of Pennsylvania, and seven honorary degrees from universities in the United States, Peru, and England. He served in the army from 1942 to 1946. Prior to retirement from Wharton in 1986, he was Chairman of the Social Systems Science Department and Director of the Busch Center for Systems Research. He has authored 23 books, the most recent of which are *Management f-Laws,* with Herbert Addison and Sally Bibb (Triarchy Press, 2007); *Idealized Design,* with Jason Magidson and Herbert J. Addison (Wharton School Publishing, 2006); *Beating the System,* with Sheldon Rovin (Berrett-Kohler, 2005); *Redesigning Society,* with Sheldon Rovin (Stanford University Press, 2003), *Re-Creating the Corporation* (Oxford University Press, 1999); *Ackoff's Best* (Wiley, 1999); and *The Democratic Corporation* (Oxford University Press, 1994). He has also published more than 200 articles in books and journals. He is a charter member and former president of the Operations Research Society of America, founding member and former vice president of the Institute of Management Sciences, and former president of the Society for General Systems Research. He has been elected a member of both the Academy of Natural Sciences for the Russian Federation and the International Academy of Management. In 2001, the Ackoff Center for the Advancement of Systems Approaches (ACASA) was established at the University of Pennsylvania in his honor. His work in research, consulting, and education has involved more than 350 corporations and 75 government agencies in the United States.

Daniel Greenberg is best known for developing a unique view of children's place in the world and implementing an innovative concept of schooling appropriate for the twenty-first century.

He has written extensively about the philosophy and practice of the unique educational environment he helped to found and develop: Sudbury Valley School, in Framingham, Massachusetts, where he has been on the staff since its inception in 1968. Many of his works help explain how to integrate conditions in the post-industrial world with a view of human nature that considers all human beings to be striving for competence (while constantly working to fashion a coherent worldview).

He works as an advisor to people developing new concepts in educational practice and fitting the ideas of participatory democracy to educational settings.

Among his publications are "Worlds in Creation," an examination of the ways individuals develop their conceptions of the world; "A New Look at Schools," an analysis of the history of education; "Education in America"; and "A Clearer View: New Insights into the Sudbury Valley School Model." He has co-authored two studies of Sudbury Valley School alumni, "Legacy of Trust" and "Pursuit of Happiness," as well as "Starting a Sudbury School." Additional groundbreaking articles on subjects ranging from the history of democratic institutions to child rearing can be found on the school's web page, www.sudval.org.

Daniel lives in the Boston suburbs. He received a Ph.D. in theoretical physics from Columbia University (1960) and served on the faculty of both the Physics and History departments there. He has published in those fields and has also worked in publishing and business. His wife, Hanna, is also a founder of Sudbury Valley School and is on the staff there. They have three children, adults now, who each attended Sudbury Valley through graduation.

Preface:
Why, and How, This Book Was Written

When we first met at a conference devoted to learning in the twenty-first century, we were delighted to find ourselves deeply in sympathy with each other's approach to education. We had each spent long years with people of all ages and in a variety of different environments—schools, universities, businesses (large and small), nonprofit organizations—espousing views that were for the most part considered radical and unrealistic. We had each endeavored to turn our dreams into reality, and we had each enjoyed enough support and success to encourage us to carry on.

But we had never crossed paths, either directly or indirectly. We soon discovered our common interests, our shared goals, and the widely divergent paths that our lives had taken. We soon became friends.

One day, we began to discuss a certain subject of mutual interest. Because we lived too far apart to meet regularly face to face, we resorted to writing each other. Because of the ease of e-mail, our exchange became, from the outset, a conversation, a rapid exchange of ideas, albeit in written rather than oral form.

The more we chatted through e-mail, the more we delved into the aspects of education that had engrossed us throughout our lives.

Eventually, this book emerged—a book we believe could be of interest to others who have struggled with the same problems.

We wanted, in the body of this book, to keep our unique voices and approaches distinct and obvious to the reader. What you will see is the actual conversation we had, rather than an amalgamation and homogenization of two separate worldviews. In each chapter, our separate views have been set off by icons to enable readers to distinguish our "voices." However, in the final section of the book, which is about our vision of ideal education, we found that we could speak with one voice, undifferentiated.

We have derived immense pleasure out of our collaboration in this venture. We hope you, the reader, will enjoy eavesdropping on our conversation.

Introduction: What Education Is About

To me education is a leading out of what is already there in the pupil's soul. ... [P]utting in of something that is not there ... is not what I call education, I call it intrusion.

—Muriel Spark

Before beginning a discussion about educational practices, it is necessary to step back and determine the central purpose of the educational enterprise. Without a clear understanding of the goals of education, it is impossible to make sensible suggestions about institutions that implement those goals.

Usually, when this subject is raised, it is dealt with through some general statement such as the following: The purpose for which schools exist is to prepare children for life in the complex world of today. The equation of education with schools, the presumption that education deals primarily with children (or with adults who have inadequate skills, and are "childlike" in this regard), and the tacit assumption that everyone knows what specific knowledge is needed in today's world—all these are treated as self-evident, and the discussion quickly moves on to details of implementation, covering such matters as curriculum, assessment, pedagogy, and current child and adult development theories.

For example, the *American Heritage Dictionary* defines education as "the act or process of imparting knowledge or skill; systematic instruction; teaching; ... schooling." How far this current definition of the term strays from its original meaning can be seen from the shorter *Oxford English Dictionary*, which begins with the definition "the process of nourishing or rearing," and refers to the Latin verb educere, from which the English word is derived, which means "to lead out," "to bring out," "to elicit," "to draw forth."

In fact, this is the meaning on which ancient Greek philosophers focused. For them, education was a lifelong process of drawing forth from within each person the full potential that lay within them. Where this potential comes from was a matter of myth, and remains, for us today, a matter of mystery. Nevertheless, the existence of some central purpose to each person's life has been a cornerstone of American thinking from the early days of the Republic. For our Founding Fathers, the notion that every human being had the "unalienable right" to "the pursuit of happiness" lay at the very core of the justification for establishing this country. This "right" meant, for them, the right to find, pursue, and realize the reason for their own existence, which gives their lives meaning, and from which they can extract satisfaction. The declaration of such a right set our fledgling nation apart from all other nations and became one of the key elements of our country's unique form of liberal democracy that has, over the intervening centuries, come to appeal to an ever-increasing number of people around the world.

For us in America, education from the outset meant the process of discovering, in each and every one of us, the meaningful endeavors to which we are willing to devote ourselves with unflagging energy, given the opportunity to do so. For us, the creation of a polity that promotes order, tolerance, peaceful coexistence, and hope for the future depends critically on the establishment of an environment in which each of the individuals who constitute the polity has been given the greatest possible opportunity to "pursue happiness" in his or her personal life. It is essential to understand this, and to keep it in the front of our consciousness when discussing education in America today.

There are several consequences to this understanding. Perhaps the most obvious is that education is, by its very nature, not a process limited to, or even primarily revolving around, childhood. It is a lifelong enterprise, and it is a process enhanced by an environment that supports—or, more precisely, "nourishes"—to the greatest extent possible the attempts of all people to "find themselves" throughout their lives. As discussed throughout this book, the dawning twenty-first century provides, in this respect, avenues that have never been hitherto available to the human race.

Something else to contemplate is the following question: Why have children been separated out as the primary objects of education in our society? Has this always been the case? If not, how has it come about, and what is the outlook for the future? In particular, is this development related to the migration of the term education from "lead forth" to "schooling"?

Actually, we know the answers to these questions. Mass schooling for all children is a recent phenomenon, a little over a century and half old. A million years of human history transpired without sending all children to formal schools—a million years during which all the world's rich cultures of prehistoric times, the ancient and medieval worlds, the Renaissance, and early "modern" times were formed, developed, and passed on. A million years during which the overwhelming majority of people lived in small, rural or tribal settings, where children from a very tender age indeed became an integral part of the larger community.[1]

Schools for children became an important feature of societies where the Industrial Revolution took hold, together with a comprehension of the challenge that industrialization might pose to the social fabric. In our modern world of computers and robotics, we tend to forget that during the first two centuries of industrialization, machines designed to produce goods at a staggering rate never before achievable through manual efforts were actually rather stupid: Their successful operation depended on the intimate conjoining of human effort to machine power. People had to perform as parts of machines—with precise, repetitive, mind-numbing action.

For societies accustomed by long tradition to having a large downtrodden underclass—such as those of Western Europe—it was not much of a challenge to transform traditional forms of servitude to the newer servitude to the machine and the company owner. For the United States, the situation was touchier. Here, a culture declaring itself to be the protector of individual liberty, and affording seemingly boundless opportunities for the expression of personal freedom, the challenge of creating a large, docile population that would accept the dominance of the factory system in their lives was enormous.[2] In the first decades of the nineteenth century, it became clear that the only way to succeed with industrializing (and hence modernizing) this country was to find a way to break the inherently free human spirit during childhood.

This was no secret, sinister conspiracy against humanity. On the contrary, it was a project discussed openly and candidly by the leading American thinkers of the day, who set out to create an environment for children in which they could be forcibly trained to be obedient, to follow orders, and to perform highly monotonous tasks without rebelling. What amounted to incarceration of children during a period of indoctrination and training was explained as a necessity for their own future good—for their own prosperity, for the prosperity of the country, and for the benefit of a glowing destiny for their progeny.

The founders of modern mass schooling decided, in addition, to use the time children spent in school to impart to them, through endless drill, some skills that were deemed useful in a thriving industrial environment. The three Rs—reading, writing, arithmetic—were seen to provide a work force that could understand basic instructions, engage in rudimentary written communication, and perform simple office functions, thus creating the most skilled mass workforce in the world.

The success of mass schooling in this country was dramatic, by industrial standards. From a provincial backwater, America rapidly marched to the forefront of industrial powers, reaching unheard-of levels of production and wealth. The mass schooling methods of child education thus appeared to be vindicated and became models for the developed world.

When we are discussing the creation of an ideal educational environment, the fundamental question before us is this: Can the root meaning of education, as a lifelong process of self-discovery, be restored in a liberal democracy such as ours in the twenty-first century? If it can, what transformations does that demand in our present culture?

Education, as currently provided, has many objectives, some conscious and some not. One objective seldom raised to consciousness is to ensure maintenance and preservation of the status quo—to produce members of society who will not challenge any fundamental aspects of the way things are. Students and teachers may be aware of the possibility of—and even favor—certain improvements, but these tend to be ones that are small and incremental, not fundamental. Some well-known aphorisms reflect this: Let well enough alone, don't rock the boat, and let nature take its course. When action is required, people tend to look for the least that needs to be done to take care of the problem.

Education has the objective of giving meaning to the lives of the students. This requires making them aware of the value they can create for others, how they can be useful to and be valued by others. This objective is enclosed in what I believe should be the primary objective of education:

to enable students to develop and be able to contribute to the development of the society of which they are part.

Unfortunately, development and growth are commonly treated as synonyms. They are not the same thing. Either can take place without the other. Rubbish heaps grow but do not develop, and Einstein continued to develop long after he stopped growing.

Growth is an increase in size or number. The amount of resources one has available can grow and is reflected in standard of living. Development is not a matter of how much one has but of how much one can do with whatever one has. This is reflected in quality of life. Robinson Crusoe is a better model of development than J. Pierpont Morgan.

To develop is to increase one's desire and ability to satisfy one's own needs and legitimate desires and those of others. A legitimate desire is one the satisfaction of which does not reduce the desire and ability of others to develop.

Development is a matter of learning, increasing one's competence. Therefore, because one cannot learn for another, the only kind of development that is possible is self-development. Others, like the educational system, can and should encourage and facilitate the self-development of students.

Development has four aspects: scientific, economic, ethical, and esthetic. Science consists of the pursuit of understanding of natural phenomena. Technology is the application of the products of science, and education is the principal means by which the outputs of science and technology are disseminated. The economy is concerned with the pursuit of plenty, making available the resources that enable people to use the outputs of science and technology. Ethics is concerned with the pursuit of the good, peace on Earth and peace of mind. This implies doing nothing to obstruct the development of others (to the contrary, promoting it). Esthetics is concerned with the pursuit of beauty and fun—the products of creative and recreative activities. Together, these four aspects make possible the continual pursuit of development, which strives toward a goal, "omni-competence," that can never be attained. However, one can always come closer to it.

Put another way, education has both extrinsic and intrinsic functions. Its extrinsic or instrumental function is to encourage and facilitate the development of students and help make them helpful to others and self-supporting members of society. It should enable them to learn what they need to know and understand to make a living and contribute to the survival of the communities of which they are part. Education's intrinsic function is to enable its subjects to derive satisfaction from activities that have no instrumental value—cultural and recreational activities such as enjoying music, art, and literature and engaging in recreational games.

Industrialization and urbanization in the United States were brought about primarily by scientific, technological, and economic advances early in the nineteenth century. Because of this, education has focused on these aspects of growth and development and given little attention to ethics and esthetics. As a result, the Industrial Revolution did a great deal of harm and created a great deal of ugliness, both of which we tend to overlook or underestimate.

In the early part of the nineteenth century, the United States was a nation of widely dispersed farms and small villages; it did not have markets large enough to support industrialization. Unlike Europe, which already had population concentrations in close geographic proximity, industrialization in the United States required two technological developments before it could take place: first, transportation that aggregated small towns and villages into larger markets, which occurred with the development of railroads; second, the ability to communicate among markets rapidly and effectively. This was accomplished by the invention of the telegraph, followed by the telephone and wireless devices.

Machines that replaced man as a source of energy, replaced his muscle, became the idols worshiped at the time. This was set forth graphically in the work of Frederick W. Taylor,[3] who by analysis reduced manual labor to simple elementary tasks that required repetitive machine-like behavior from unskilled laborers.

As industrialization progressed, work and the mechanization associated with it became more complex. More skill and knowledge were required from workers. Schools extended their offerings into the challenge. Technical and professional schools emerged and flourished. Also, as industrialization expanded, and particularly with the demand for labor during the world wars, women were drawn into the workplace They were liberated; children were left in the care of others and the educational system. This imposed on schools a new function: "baby (and older child) sitting."

The economic success of mechanized production raised the concept of the factory to an elevated position in society. It suggested to educators that they design and operate schools as much like factories as possible. Students came to be thought of as raw material to be processed mechanically into "salable" finished products.

Our society has now entered another era called, among other things, the post-industrial era. The educational system has yet to catch up with this transformation. Perhaps the essence of this transformation was best capsulized by Einstein when he wrote, "One should guard against preaching to young people success in the customary form as the main aim in life. The most important motive for work in school and in life is pleasure in work, pleasure in its result, and the knowledge of the value of the result to the community." Such a universal statement could only have been made in a post-industrial world.

PART 1

Where Today's Educational System Fails

Soap and education are not as sudden as a massacre,
but they are more deadly in the long run.

—Mark Twain

1

Learning and Teaching

Education is an admirable thing, but it is well to remember from time to time that nothing that is worth learning can be taught.

—Oscar Wilde

Confusing Learning with Teaching

Traditional education focuses on teaching, not learning. It incorrectly assumes that for every ounce of teaching there is an ounce of learning by those who are taught. However, most of what we learn before, during, and after attending schools is learned without it being taught to us. A child learns such fundamental things as how to walk, talk, eat, dress, and so on without being taught these things. Adults learn most of what they use at work or at leisure while at work or leisure. Most of what is taught in classroom settings is forgotten, and much or what is remembered is irrelevant.

In most schools, memorization is mistaken for learning. Most of what is remembered is remembered only for a short time, but then is quickly forgotten. (How many remember how to find a square root or ever have a need to?) Furthermore, even young children are aware of the fact that most of what is expected of them in school can better be done by computers, recording machines, cameras, and so on. They are treated as poor surrogates for such machines and instruments. Why should children— or adults, for that matter—be asked to do something computers and

---

related equipment can do much better than they can? Why doesn't education focus on what humans can do better than the machines and instruments they create?

When those who have taught others are asked who in the classes learned most, virtually all of them say, "The teacher." It is apparent to those who have taught that teaching is a better way to learn than being taught. Teaching enables the teacher to discover what one thinks about the subject being taught. Schools are upside down: Students should be teaching and faculty learning.[4]

After lecturing to undergraduates at a major university, I was accosted by a student who had attended the lecture. After some complimentary remarks, he asked, "How long ago did you teach your first class?"

I responded, "In September of 1941."

"Wow!" The student said. "You mean to say you have been teaching for more than 60 years?"

"Yes."

"When did you last teach a course in a subject that existed when you were a student?"

This difficult question required some thought. After a pause, I said, "September of 1951."

"Wow! You mean to say that everything you have taught in more than 50 years was not taught *to* you; you had to learn on your own?"

"Right."

"You must be a pretty good learner."

I modestly agreed.

The student then said, "What a shame you're not that good a teacher."

The student had it right; what most faculty members are good at, if anything, is learning rather than teaching. Recall that in the one-room schoolhouse, students taught students. The teacher served as a guide and a resource but not as one who force-fed content into students' minds.

There are many different ways of learning; teaching is only one of them. We learn a great deal on our own, in independent study or play. We learn a great deal interacting with others informally—sharing what we are learning with others and vice versa. We learn a great deal by doing, through trial and error. Long before there were schools as we know them, there was apprenticeship—learning how to do something by trying it under the guidance of one who knows how. For example, one can learn more architecture by having to design and build one's own house than by taking any number of courses on the subject. When physicians are asked whether they learned more in classes or during their internship, without exception they answer, "Internship."

In the educational process, students should be offered a wide variety of ways to learn, among which they could choose or with which they could experiment. They do not have to learn different things the same way. They should learn at a very early stage of "schooling" that learning how to learn is largely their responsibility—with the help they seek but that is not imposed on them.

The objective of education is learning, not teaching.

There are two ways that teaching is a powerful tool of learning. Let's abandon for the moment the loaded word "teaching," which is unfortunately all too closely linked to the notion of "talking at" or "lecturing," and use instead the rather awkward phrase, "explaining something to someone else who wants to find out about it." One aspect of explaining something is getting yourself up to snuff on whatever it is that you are trying to explain. I can't very well explain to you how Newton accounted for planetary motion if I haven't boned up on my Newtonian mechanics first. This is a problem we all face all the time, when we are expected to explain something. (Wife asks, "How do we get to Valley Forge from home?" And husband, who does not want to admit he has no idea at all, excuses himself to go to the bathroom; he quickly Googles MapQuest to find out.) This is one sense in which the one who explains learns the most, because the person to whom the explanation is made can afford to forget the explanation promptly in most cases; but the explainers will find it sticking in their minds a lot longer, because they struggled to gain an understanding in the first place in a form clear enough to explain.

The second aspect of explaining something that leaves the explainer more enriched, and with a much deeper understanding of the subject, is this: To satisfy the person being addressed, to the point where that person can nod his head and say, "Ah, yes, now I understand!" explainers must not only get the matter to fit comfortably into their own worldview (that is, into their own personal frame of reference for understanding the world around them), but they also have to figure out how to link their frame of reference to the worldview of the person receiving the explanation so that the explanation can make sense to that person, too. This involves an intense effort on the part of the explainer to get into the other person's mind, so to speak, and that exercise is at the heart of learning in general. For, by practicing repeatedly how to create links between my mind and another's, I am reaching the very core of the art of learning from the ambient culture. Without that skill, I can only learn from direct experience; with that skill, I can learn from the experience of the whole world. Thus, whenever I struggle to explain something to someone else, and succeed in doing so, I am advancing my ability to learn from others, too.

This aspect of learning through explanation has been overlooked by most commentators. And that is a shame, because both aspects of learning are what makes the age mixing that takes place in the world at large such a valuable educational tool. Younger kids are always seeking answers from older kids—sometimes just slightly older kids (the 7 year old tapping the presumed life wisdom of the so-much-more-experienced 9 year old), often much older kids. The older kids love it, and their abilities are exercised mightily in these interactions. They have to figure out what it is that they understand about the question being raised, and they have to figure out how to make their understanding comprehensible to the younger kids. The same process occurs over and over again in the world at large; this is why it is so important to keep communities multi-aged, and why it is so destructive to learning, and to the development of culture in general, to segregate certain ages (children, old people) from others.

What went on in the one-room schoolhouse is much like what I have been talking about. In fact, I am not sure that the adult teacher in the one-room schoolhouse was always viewed as the best authority on any given subject! Long ago, I had an experience that illustrates that point perfectly. When our oldest son was 8 years old, he hung around (and virtually worshiped) a very brilliant 13 year old named Ernie, who loved science. Our son was curious about everything in the world. One day he asked me to explain some physical phenomenon that lay within the realm of what we have come to call "physics"; being a former professor of physics, I was considered a reasonable person to ask. So, I gave him an answer—the "right" answer, the one he would have found in books. He was greatly annoyed. "That's not right!" he shouted, and when I expressed surprise at his response and asked him why he would say so, his answer was immediate: "Ernie said so and so, which is totally different, and Ernie knows." It was an enlightening and delightful experience for me. It was clear that his faith in Ernie had been developed over a long time, from long experience with Ernie's unfailing ability to build a bridge between their minds—perhaps more successfully, at least in certain areas, than I had been.

One might wonder how on earth learning came to be seen primarily a result of teaching. Until quite recently, the world's great teachers were understood to be people who had something fresh to say about something to people who were interested in hearing their message. Moses, Socrates, Aristotle, Jesus—these were people who had original insights, and people came from far and wide to find out what those insights were. One can see most clearly in Plato's dialogues that people did not come to Socrates to "learn philosophy," but rather to hear Socrates' version of philosophy (and his wicked and witty attacks on other people's versions), just as they went to other philosophers to hear (and learn) their versions. In other words, teaching was understood as public exposure of an individual's perspective, which anyone could take or leave, depending on whether they cared about it.

No one in his right mind thought that the only way you could become a philosopher was by taking a course from one of those guys. On the contrary, you were expected to come up with your own original worldview if you aspired to the title of philosopher. This was true of any and every aspect of knowledge; you figured out how to learn it, and you exposed yourself to people who were willing to make their understanding public if you thought it could be a worthwhile part of your endeavor. That is the basis for the formation of universities in the Middle Ages—places where thinkers were willing to spend their time making their thoughts public. The only ones who got to stay were the ones whom other people ("students") found relevant enough to their own personal quests to make listening to them worthwhile.

By the way, this attitude toward teaching has not disappeared. When quantum theory was being developed in the second quarter of the twentieth century, aspiring atomic physicists traveled to the various places where different theorists were developing their thoughts, often in radically different directions. Students traveled to Bohr's institute to find out how he viewed quantum theory, then to Heisenberg, to Einstein, to Schrodinger, to Dirac, and so on. What was true of physics was equally true of art, architecture…you name it. It is still true today. One does not go to Pei to learn "architecture"; one goes to learn how he does it—that is, to see him "teach" by telling and showing you his approach. Schools should enable people to go where they want to go, not where others want them to.

The trouble began when mass education was introduced. It was necessary

- To decide what skills and knowledge everyone has to have to be a productive citizen of a developed country in the industrial age

- To make sure the way this information is defined and standardized, to fit into the standardization required by the industrial culture

- To develop the means of describing and communicating the standardized information (textbooks, curricula)

- To train people to comprehend the standardized material and master the means of transmitting it (teacher training, pedagogy)

- To create places where the trainees (children) and the trainers (unfortunately called "teachers," which gives them a status they do not deserve) can meet—so-called "schools" (again a term stolen from a much different milieu, endowing these new institutions with a dignity they also do not deserve)

- And, to provide the coercive backing necessary to carry out this major cultural and social upheaval

In keeping with all historic attempts to revolutionize the social order, the elite leaders who formulated the strategy, and those who implemented it, perverted the language, using terms that had attracted a great deal of respect in new ways that turned their meanings upside down, but helped make the new order palatable to a public that didn't quite catch on. Every word—*teacher, student, school, discipline,* and so on—took on meanings diametrically opposed to what they had originally meant.

Consider this one example from my recent experience. I attended a conference of school counselors, where the latest ideas in the realm of student counseling were being presented. I went to a session on the development of self-discipline and responsibility, wondering what these concepts mean to people embedded in traditional schooling. To me, self-discipline means the ability to pursue one's goals without outside coercion; responsibility means taking appropriate action on one's own initiative, without being goaded by others. To the people presenting the session, both concepts had to do solely with the child's ability to do his or her assigned classwork. They explained that a guidance counselor's proper function was to get students to understand that responsible behavior meant doing their homework in a timely and effective manner, as prescribed, and self-discipline meant the determination to get that homework done. George Orwell was winking in the back of the room.

Today, there are two worlds that use the word *education* with opposite meanings: One world consists of the schools and colleges (and even graduate schools) of our education complex, in which standardization prevails. In that world, an industrial training megastructure strives to turn out identical replicas of a product called "people educated for the twenty-first century." The second is the world of information, knowledge, and wisdom, in which the real population of the world resides when not incarcerated in schools. In that world, learning takes place like it always did, and teaching consists of imparting one's wisdom, among other things, to voluntary listeners.

This is how I think about some of the words used in the context of education:

- By *teaching* I mean transmission of information, knowledge, understanding, or wisdom to another by speech (usually lecturing) or the written word (as in a textbook) This is fundamentally one-way communication. Q&A is not discussion but a way of expanding teaching in the sense previously stated. Teaching informs, instructs, explains, or enlightens. Explanations transmit understanding. Enlightenment transmits wisdom.

- By *instruction* I mean transmission of knowledge, how to do something, by word of mouth or in writing, frequently accompanied by illustration (by the instructor doing it).

- By *training* I mean inculcating in another a specific act or set of actions to be repeated often. This is by word of mouth or in writing and often accompanied by examples of doing it.

  The difference between instruction and training is subtle but very important. I can instruct you on how to drive a car without ever driving one or having you do so. But, if I train you to drive, I will have you drive until you can do it independently. Therefore, training is instruction plus trials, application.

- When two or more parties share what they know or understand in discussion, I think of this as *exposure.* To present something for acceptance or rejection by others is *to discuss.*

- *Wisdom* is neither taught, nor instructed, nor trained. It is imparted, put up for grabs. It cannot be imposed or taught by rote.

Education includes all of the above. Education need not involve words, although it usually does. In an apprenticeship (for instance, in a painting or sculpture studio), learning may take place just by seeing how another does it. Of course, words may supplement observation significantly.

Intelligence is the ability to learn, not a measure of how much one has learned.

Motivating Learning

No matter how "good" the teaching or the opportunities to learn, an unmotivated student learns nothing. Motivated students and adults learn without being taught; they do so by means they select. For example, the American Statistical Association once conducted a survey of its membership to determine which four contemporary statisticians were considered to be the most important contributors to the field. The four persons selected addressed the anniversary celebration of the association. Not one had ever had a course in statistics. In each case, they had wanted to solve a problem that required the use of statistical methods that did not exist at the time, and so they invented new ones.

The power of motivation is illustrated by the following story. The leader of a poor inner-city neighborhood found that the vast majority of minority children coming out of primary school were functionally illiterate. The board of education's special unit on literacy had been called in but had no effect. The community's leader then sought help from a professor at a local university who had no experience with literacy problems. The leader explained that because experts could not help with the problem, maybe an outsider could.

Having worked in that neighborhood on other problems, the professor knew the young people were not dumb; to the contrary, they were incredibly street smart. Therefore, he suspected the reading deficiency was due to lack of motivation, not intelligence. Aided by graduate students, he conducted a door-to-door survey of households in the community to find out how many contained a book. More than 65 percent didn't. Furthermore, he discovered that most of the children entering school had rarely, if ever, been read to by a parent or another adult (or even seen someone read).

The culture in which they had grown up was orally oriented, not literary. Rap was an invention of that culture.

With funds obtained from the Sears Foundation, the professor purchased a set of Charlie Chaplin's silent films and had them shown during every school day in the primary school's auditorium. Students were permitted to sit in on the films at will. In a very short time, the desire for literacy permeated the school, and learning began. The students desperately wanted to read the titles in the films.

We are motivated to learn when we see those we admire and respect, even love (for example, parents), engaged in an activity that brings them great satisfaction. We try to emulate them. Faculty can serve as role models—it is in that sense that they are the most effective motivators. But then they have to be seen learning, not only teaching. Today, this is much more likely to be seen at a university where faculty are engaged in research, and students can participate in it with them. But, why does this have to be reserved for higher education? Anyone who has no desire to learn should have no involvement in the learning of others.

There can be little doubt that self-initiated learning that arises from the internal motivation of the learner is the most efficient and best retained type of learning, least likely to arouse resistance or encounter seemingly insurmountable blocks. The question of whence motivation arises is, however, a much more controversial and critical one.

The common view, one that underpins almost all educational enterprises that have arisen over the past 150 years, is that motivation must be instilled from without, by a pedagogically sophisticated educator. This view is understandable when education is considered a way to enforce a particular social agenda on children. From the realization that such coercion inevitably arouses antagonism came the need to convince children that society's agenda is actually their own agenda, too; only then would children in school be able to learn effectively. The primary activity of schooling became pedagogy, instilling in children motivation to do what the school authorities wanted them to do (or, in plainer terms, seducing children to think they love spinach by looking for ways to cook it that would make it seem delicious to them).

The reason this has been such a dismal failure, especially as the information age unfolds, is that seduction is ultimately a poor tool for a long-term relationship—in this case, between a person and an area of study. A poignant story illustrates the point. As a young professor of physics, I worked hard to develop a set of inspirational lectures, all carefully crafted to motivate the undergraduates in my introductory course to learn a subject that was widely considered to be too hard and too dull for most students. One day, a senior walked into the office and asked to speak with me. "You have ruined my life," the senior said, with more sadness than anger. "How?" I asked. "When I was a freshman, I took your course. You made physics so interesting that I decided to major in it. It wasn't until my senior year that I realized that I am actually not really interested in the subject, and that my talents and goals lie elsewhere. Because of you, my entire college career was wasted."

In fact, pedagogical seduction that works is the exception rather than the rule. Most of the time, it just fails from the get-go.

Whence, then, does internal motivation come from, if not from someone on the outside looking for ways to instill it? The fact is that our present state of knowledge does not allow us to answer this crucial question. The source of our internally driven life goals and passions remains a mystery. Some would trace it to genetics, some to parental or family influence, some to peers, some to exposure to role models, some to random life experiences, some to supernatural inspiration. Whatever its source, its existence is undeniable and often visible from earliest childhood.

Consider the following true anecdote. One day we took our 2-year-old son for an outing to a local city zoo. We were planning something guaranteed to give him pleasure; after all, what child doesn't enjoy a zoo? He liked looking at pictures of animals in books, and he knew we were on our way to see live animals. No sooner had we alighted from the bus than he noticed the cobblestone sidewalk in front of the zoo entrance and promptly sat down to study its patterns. For well over an hour, he was wholly engrossed in looking intensely at cobblestones. We never got into the zoo.

Where did this passion for patterns come from? Certainly not from anything he had heretofore encountered, as far as we knew. It was a new delight, offered to him purely by chance, and one that resonated with something deep within him. As a young man, he became a passionate art photographer, focusing in particular on the myriad patterns that the world around him offered. How did this determined internal motivation arise?

Most people have similar, possibly less-eccentric, stories in their lives. The key role of an educational system devoted to enabling children to develop their interests is to provide a setting in which the various internal motivations each child possesses can flourish into active pursuits. It is not the role of adults to attempt to replace the motivations already present in children with others that the adults wish the children had.

What, then, are we to make of the instance cited previously, where the clever introduction of Chaplin silent movies motivated children to learn? A closer look at the story yields a different take on the situation. The adult agenda was to find a way to motivate children to learn to read. The reason the adults pursued this agenda was twofold: First, all the attempts made in the primary school classrooms had so far failed to instill literacy in the children; and, second, the adults were of the firm conviction that every person had to know how to read to function minimally in today's world, and that something had to be done actively to make sure children will be able to read.

Why all the attempts made in the classrooms failed should be clear from what I have already said. But what of the second point? Underlying it is the tacit assumption that, left on their own, children will not discover that this crucial element of modern adult life exists. It is somehow a "mystery" that adults know but that is hidden from children.

Suppose, however, that these same children who were exposed to the Chaplin films in movie sessions (that were, to say the least, welcome reprieves from the unspeakable boredom of classroom work) were allowed to encounter the world around them freely during the day, instead of being forced to sit in classes. If, indeed, some level of reading is critical to functioning in the world, what are the odds that children would not find this out on their own? Don't they figure out and ultimately master myriad other critical features of adult life (such as speech, social skills, using a phone or computer, driving, and so forth)? After all, reading is a simple matter of decoding a few symbols that represent spoken language. Why assume it is beyond their abilities to do on their own initiative, when they discover a need for reading on their own and are internally motivated to do so? When so motivated, they require access to printed and written material.[5]

In fact, many schools exist that have done away with reading instruction altogether; those schools allow children to come to that skill when they seek it on their own. It should surprise no one to find out that eventually all the children become readers sooner or later—some at the age of 4, some at the age of 12!—and that so-called "reading disorders" are extremely rare in such schools.

Computers and Education

Educators tout the value of computers and the Internet in their schools, primarily because they have heard that these are the tools of the future, and they want to appear modern and up-to-date. So, they bring the hardware into the schools—and then they use it in lieu of, and just like, the standard hard-copy textbooks and workbooks of old. They impose stringent limits on students' free access to these electronic paraphernalia and prescribe in detail how, where, when, and for what purpose students are to use them.

The fact is, however, that through the cyberworld, people of all ages can now link themselves directly to the most up-to-date sources of information on virtually any topic they choose to pursue. In other words, a person who wants to find out about something now has the ability to seek out world-class expertise, to access it at will, and to follow it up to whatever level of excellence desired. *There is no way that the vast majority of teachers, whatever their training, can ever hope to match in their class-rooms what students can receive at will from sources of their own choosing.* In addition, it is a simple matter for any person to link up with others having the same interests, anywhere in the world, and to engage in mutually enriching conversations and interactions that further enhance the understanding of all the participants.

No less significant is the almost infinite diversity of activities and interests accessible to all children—a diversity that stands in stark contrast to the narrowly limited field of view presented by the handful of subjects selected by anonymous pedagogues as the proper focus for all students. *By comparison to the wealth of variety available on the Internet, on CDs, on DVDs, and on a host of other storage media, the world of traditional education seems hopelessly sterile, arcane, and irrelevant.* No person who has surfed the web can ever turn back to the dry pages of a textbook, or the dry elements of a class assignment, without realizing how exciting the former is, and how drab the latter.

Even more significant is the total age irrelevance of cyberspace. Logging on does not entail disclosing your age. (Nor, for that matter, does it disclose your gender, religion, race, ethnic origin, or any other factor that has, for so long, played a major role in determining a person's relationship with those around them.) Everyone in cyberspace is a *person,* and what she or he says is, perforce, treated in the same manner as the communication of any other person.

But how can people learn to engage this new electronic universe? Don't they have to be taught the relevant techniques?

Once again, we encounter the importance of providing an environment in which accessibility, not instruction, is the chief factor. Nothing illustrates this better than an amazing experiment carried out several years ago in India by Sugata Mitra, a physicist by training, who headed the Research and Development department of the Indian Institute of Technology in Delhi. It all began when he started thinking about the following common phenomenon, all too well known to most of us past the age of 30. In his own words: "Any parent who had given his child a computer would invariably remark to me about it. I could hardly ever find an exception. Within a very short period of time, the parent would be claiming that the child was a genius with a computer. When I poked a little further, I invariably found that the child was doing things with the computer that the parent didn't understand."

This led Mitra to the following outlandish experiment. His institute is a beautiful building set adjacent to some of Delhi's worst slums. Mitra had a hole drilled in the outside wall of the institute, and placed in it a computer with a high-speed connection to the Internet. There was a touchpad, but no keyboard. All that showed was the opening screen of MSN.com. And that was it. There was no adult around to help, and no set of instructions nearby to guide anyone who might care to consult them.

Very quickly, the street urchins started to explore this strange new intrusion into their world. Not one of them had any prior exposure to a computer, or even knew what a computer was. To them, this was some mysterious entity that had suddenly appeared, and that warranted the usual curiosity and exploration that they devoted to anything new that came their way. Most of the children were not even literate, and none knew English. The results were spectacular. In Mitra's words, "You get base-level computer literacy almost instantly...The ability to use the mouse, to point, to drag, to drop, to copy, and to browse the Internet."

How they did this was fascinating. Mitra continues: "The children create their own metaphors. To give you an idea of what I mean, a journalist came up to one of these kids and asked him, 'How do you know so much about computers?' The answer seemed very strange to her because the kid said, 'What's a computer?' The terminology is not as important as the metaphor." They gave different aspects of their exploration names: The mouse pointer they called "needle" in Hindi, and the hourglass that you see while a process is taking place they called "Shiva's drum," from their own mythology. They discovered Microsoft Paint and used it to draw, and later they unearthed the very obscure (and not widely known) character map that is in the Microsoft Word program, which enabled them to place letters on the screen without a keyboard! And so it went.

Mitra realized that his simple novel idea has enormous potential implications for education. He calls this approach "minimally invasive education" and defines it as "a system of education where you assume that children know how to put two and two together on their own." He adds, "Creating content is not what's important. What is important is infrastructure and access."

Twenty-five years ago, computer-assisted instruction (CAI) was considered by many to be the savior of education, but it turned out to be a fad with a short life. After the initial fascination that students had with the computer, they became bored with being taught by them. Furthermore, they came to resent a machine that knew more than they did and controlled them. Think of what it does to one's self image to be manipulated by a machine. Wasn't it supposed to be the other way around?

In fact, by putting the student in control of the computer rather than vice versa, the living student becomes a teacher of the computer. For example, in the 1960s, Professor Stuart Cooke at Case Institute of Technology in Cleveland had second graders teaching a computer arithmetic. Of course, they could not teach what they did not know. They had to design their own learning of what they were supposed to teach the computer. They did so. Their "teachers" acted as resources that the students could use however they, the students, saw fit. The students had a great time and could hardly wait to get at the computer. In addition, they learned arithmetic rapidly and remembered it long after their counterparts, who were taught but then forgot it.

Computers have also been used to enable students to learn effectively from each other, as facilitators of learning. This is demonstrated in the following experiment, which involved learning English grammar. Three tables were arranged in a triangle with a desktop computer on each. A student seated at each table could see the faces of the other two but not their screens. The computer placed on the screen of each a sentence that contained a grammatical error—for example, "The boys is hurting each other." The students were asked to touch the error with a light pen and select from a set of choices the correct replacement.

If all three students did so correctly, the computer would put the next sentence on their screens. If they were not all correct, the computer would let them know this, but not who and how many were wrong. The students had to learn this through discussion and use of references. Only when all three had gotten it right would the computer proceed to the next sentence.

The three students involved became a team that engaged in collaborative learning in other areas.

What People Learn

The content of human minds—and therefore what can be learned—falls into five classes: *data, information, knowledge, understanding,* and *wisdom.* They are not equally valuable, however, as reflected in the following aphorisms:

- An ounce of information is worth a pound of data.

- An ounce of knowledge is worth a pound of information.

- An ounce of understanding is worth a pound of knowledge.

- An ounce of wisdom is worth a pound of understanding.

Using this tongue-in-cheek metric, an ounce of wisdom is worth 65,536 ounces of data and 4,096 ounces of information. Despite this, the educational system allocates most of its time to the transmission of information, a bit to knowledge, virtually nothing to understanding, and absolutely nothing to wisdom.

Data consist of symbols that represent the properties of objects and events. For example, the address of a building uses numeric and alphabetic symbols to represent the building's location.

Information consists of data that has been processed to make it useful. Therefore, data is to information as iron ore is to iron. Nothing useful can be made out of iron ore until it has been converted into iron. Information is contained in *descriptions:* answers to questions that begin with such words as *who, where, when,* and *how many.*

Knowledge consists of answers to *how-to* questions; it is contained in *instructions.* To say New York is 92 miles to the north and slightly east of Philadelphia is to provide information. To say one can get from one to the other easily by car using the Pennsylvania and New Jersey turnpikes is to instruct, to provide knowledge—*how to* get from one place to the other.

Understanding is contained in *explanations,* answers to *why* questions. If the one providing instructions of how to go from Philadelphia to New York asks the recipient, "Why do you want to go there?" that person is asking for an explanation, and is seeking understanding of the request. Explanations consist of the *reasons* for behavior or properties.

Reasons are of two types, retrospective and prospective: identifying what produced the behavior or properties to be explained, or what that which is to be explained is intended to produce. For example, to say that a boy is going to the store because his mother sent him is a retrospective explanation. To say he is going to the store to buy food for dinner is to provide a prospective explanation.

Wisdom is qualitatively different from data, information, knowledge, and understanding. All these are concerned with *efficiency,* the probability of succeeding in getting what one is going after and the amount of resources consumed in getting there. They have nothing to do with the value or worth of what is sought. What is sought can be a very bad thing. (One can seek to commit genocide more efficiently, for instance.) Wisdom takes the value of what is sought into account. It is captured in Peter Drucker's distinction between doing things right (*efficiency*) and doing the right thing (*effectiveness*).

Wisdom is concerned with both the long-term and the short-term consequences of what we do. It yields a willingness to make short-term sacrifices for longer-term gains. It diminishes the pressure for instant gratification and, therefore, makes the pursuit of ideals and long-run objectives possible.

Our educational system ignores these distinctions, and as a result offers scant opportunity for people to develop wisdom. Why is this important? First and foremost, it is important because most of the serious social and institutional problems that confront us are the result of trying to do the wrong things "righter." Acquiring wisdom is prerequisite to correcting the deficiencies in our society.

For example, consider the health-care system in the United States. It is widely recognized as being dysfunctional in several respects. According to Drs. Welch, Schwartz, and Woloshin, "For most Americans, the biggest health threat is not avian flu, West Nile virus, or mad cow disease. It is our health-care system."[6]

About 47 million people have no health-care coverage in the United States. The costs are increasing faster than the production of wealth. Therefore, it consumes an increasing share of the wealth produced in the United States. Why? Because it is primarily occupied with caring for the sick and disabled, not the healthy, and because the servers derive the bulk of their income, if not all of it, from service to the sick and disabled.

The way they are compensated is wrong, and as long as it remains, so will the system's dysfunctionality. Health-care providers should be paid for keeping people healthy; in turn, they should be asked to pay the costs associated with servicing people's sickness or disability. This would provide a powerful incentive, now lacking in the health-care system, for keeping people healthy (instead of waiting until they are sick or disabled to "treat" them).[7]

A striking example of the difference between doing the wrong things "righter," as opposed to doing the right things "wrong" and learning from mistakes,[8] is the approach taken by the most highly trained military minds in the various countries that participated in World War I. Although the American Civil War had revealed in stark detail the dead end that traditional military doctrine had reached, European generals and planners paid no attention to what had transpired in what was considered a cultural backwater far removed from the advanced practices of the Old World. Therefore, when confronted with the stalemated trench warfare of the chief theater of operations, the Western Front, army leaders of the main belligerents—France, England, Austria, and Germany—responded by pressing forward to do the wrong thing better and better and better.

The extent of the disaster that this approach visited upon Europe cannot be exaggerated. During a period of four years, nations that considered themselves to be the standard-bearers of the world's most enlightened civilization methodically slaughtered the better part of their youth. Several lines of deep and intricate trench system were dug by the Allies and the Central Powers across the entire length of the French border from Switzerland to the Atlantic Ocean. The traditional strategy of frontal warfare (there were no flanks to turn) and the traditional tactics of mass assault were applied without consideration of their increasing ineffectiveness in the face of the more powerful firepower possessed by the infantry, the greater destructiveness of modern artillery, and the more advanced technology of underground defense systems. Month after month, year after year, the same old massed assaults were launched—this time with heavier advanced bombardment, that time with larger numbers of troops—always with the same devastating outcomes. In the battles over Verdun alone—one small sector in the front—well over a million casualties were inflicted on both sides during more than a year of fruitless struggle.

Doing the wrong thing better and better led, inevitably and inexorably, to getting worse and worse outcomes. It took a creative, highly unpopular maverick political leader to conceive of the right thing to do in this situation and to tenaciously back those who would develop this conception into reality. Winston Churchill fell in love with the tank, in effect a moving fortress with the ability to traverse trenches. Mocked by nearly the entire military establishment, he stubbornly supported the development of this complex new weapon and all but forced the front-line generals to use it.

And what a disaster the first attempts to use the right thing were! Conceived as a decisive weapon to turn the tide of battle, the usefulness of the tank was dependent (as Churchill clearly saw) on surprise and on its use en masse. The resistant generals, however, not willing to do the right thing right, employed surprise (they couldn't help themselves; after all, the tank was a new weapon no one on either side had ever seen before) but used only a small number of tanks initially, allegedly to "test the waters." This was a case of doing the right thing very wrong!

Eventually, doing the right thing, tactically and strategically, worked its way into twentieth-century military thinking, and armored warfare became an accepted aspect of doctrine. Although neither war itself nor the propensity to use force as an integral feature of international relations was eliminated, the duration of battles shortened considerably, and the number of casualties on the battlefield declined precipitously.

Little effort is made in the world of education today to encourage the development of wisdom. The center-pin of current education is information, masses of information, represented as the essential components of knowledge, which itself is highly regarded. Understanding is considered on occasion, wisdom hardly at all. This is a critical failing.

When all is said and done, it is wisdom that we seek more than anything and that we wish our fellow citizens to possess. We want them to be able to make value judgments, to know the consequences of their (and others') actions, and to learn from their mistakes.

The only way to develop values and judgment about one's actions is to be able to exercise judgment and apply values in everyday life, in a way that is meaningful and relevant to you. Wisdom is not something that one teaches in a course (or even through the lectures of a person we acknowledge to be wise). If we honestly seek out the sources of wisdom of a person we admire, we may absorb some of the experience and attitude that inform that person's life. But to be wise is to own wisdom, as yours, not as someone else's, and to do that one must constantly be faced with situations that call for the practice and application of wisdom—in school, at work, and throughout life.

2

The Classroom Environment

What does education often do? It makes a straight-cut ditch of a free, meandering brook.

—Henry David Thoreau

Testing

In the world outside of classrooms, the "real world," examinations are seldom used to determine the competence of people. Employees are usually evaluated by how well they perform on their jobs. In the real world, ability to use what is known in dealing with real situations is the way people should be and usually are evaluated, not by how much of what they are told they can regurgitate.

Schools at every level attempt to determine, if not measure, how much students have learned by use of examinations, tests. These give questions to be answered, exercises to be completed, or problems to be solved. They expect the student to work in complete isolation with access to no resources other than his own mind. No cribbing or use of others ("cheating") is permitted. In effect, students are examined while in (what is effectively) solitary confinement. This scenario is diametrically opposed to what is expected of them in the real world.

When adults are given a problem, they are seldom required to solve it without assistance or use of external resources. But, they are expected to be able to find and acquire whatever is needed to handle the problem. What is called "cheating" in school is, in the world outside of school, a

---

highly valued ability to use external resources effectively. One who can solve fewer problems without help but more problems with help is more valuable that one who has the reverse property. Students in school, however, get little opportunity to learn how to use external resources to solve real problems. They have to learn this surreptitiously. If nothing else, schools should encourage and facilitate learning how to use external resources in dealing with "reality."

Students in school do not learn that problems, exercises, and questions are very different and that all three are abstractions from reality. (These are discussed later in this chapter in the "Solving Problems" section.) Focusing on them as preparation for life is like learning how to box with one arm tied behind your back. There is trouble when a person so trained is put in a ring with an opponent who has two hands free, even an opponent who is not very good at boxing.

Recently, the federal government introduced a set of "standards" to be met by schools if they want to receive federal financial support. These standards involve the average scores obtained by students in examinations that they must take at different grade levels.[9] Those schools whose average student scores do not meet the standards are subject to "punishment."

Obviously, this process assumes that the tests measure what is learned by the students taking them. This belief is based on the assumption that all children undergo the same developmental process, at the same basic rate, from birth until maturity. Under this assumption, all first graders are called upon to engage in the same activities; all second graders are called upon to engage in another, different set of materials and be tested on them; and so on for other grades.

The underlying assumption on which this strategy is based is wholly contradicted by the experiential reality of child development. The reality is that every child has his or her own highly specific and original way of growing up. No two siblings, no two identical twins, have ever developed the same exact way over their childhood years. This diversity begins at birth—indeed, even in the womb—and never stops until we die.

To deny this diversity is to deny the very existence of individuality. To acknowledge this diversity and nevertheless insist that each child be treated as if he or she is developmentally similar is to deny every child the right to grow up expressing his or her individuality to its fullest extent. The age of drones, who do what they are told and accept the robotic demands of the industrial era, is gone and over with.

In the name of "raising standards," the education-reform movement that has gripped the country has instituted the most rigorous implementation of lock-step teaching ever known in the world of education. The new educational order all but eliminates the possibility of children pursuing their individual interests, or learning different things from their peers, or advancing at different rates from others their age. The new educational order also all but eliminates the opportunity for teachers to teach to their strengths, to impart their special enthusiasms, to develop unique and diverse relationships with each of their students. It eliminates the possibility of significant experimentation by talented principals or school administrators, and makes it all but impossible for a local school board to try out alternative approaches in special school environments. Creativity, innovation, and individuality can no longer be afforded by anyone under education reform because the cost of poor performance on standardized tests is failure for all parties involved.

A cornerstone of the entire standardized testing movement is the conviction that these tests are a useful tool for measuring something significant about a person's ability to perform a task with proficiency, that they assess something meaningful about children. In particular, because the whole point of schooling is to prepare children to be effective adults in the society at large, the tests are supposed to be significant tools in determining whether a child is developing in a manner that will lead them toward a productive life as an adult.

If there is one thing that everybody knows, it is this: There is no way to measure in advance, by written test or any other instrument, whether a person will succeed in a given undertaking. I say that "everybody knows" this for a fact, although most people don't realize that they know it. Think about it. If there was a way to design an advance assessment that would tell us whether a person will be a successful entrepreneur, or manager, or secretary, or journalist, or carpenter, or auto mechanic, or artist, or physician, or lawyer, or anything else, every single employer and institution in the country would use such an assessment with joy! It would eliminate all need to worry about the complex process of evaluating potential employees. It would eliminate the doubts, the questions, the worries, and the failures. One could whip out an assessment packet, administer it to the prospect, and—voilà!—hire only the ones who passed, with the assurance that the position will be filled by a competent worker!

Let's be clear about this. There are, of course, tests that measure very specific skills that a person has—for example, the ability to type accurately at a certain speed, the ability to use a word processing program, the ability to handle tools properly, the ability to remember the provisions of the plumbing code. These are highly specialized, narrowly focused skills that may be requirements for specific jobs. There are hundreds of such skills, and they are all specific to particular types of work. Tests that measure these skills can tell you whether the person tested has them, and to what degree. However, the tests do not tell you anything about the ability of the person who possesses these narrow skills to perform the job for which the person is applying. Knowing how to type well doesn't make a good secretary, or writer; knowing how to handle tools properly doesn't make a good craftsman.

Nor has anybody suggested that such narrowly defined skills be possessed by everyone. It is absurd to suggest that every child who graduates high school must be able to be a good typist, to pass the Mr. Goodwrench exam, to play piano exercises flawlessly, to know the plumbing code, and so forth. This is because everyone realizes that these skills are specialized and are needed only by specialists.

But beyond such narrow tests, no method has ever been devised to assess the broader abilities that really count in life—such complex characteristics as judgment, honesty, intellectual curiosity, creativity, self-motivation, initiative, persistence, intensity, interpersonal skills, and the many other such personal traits that distinguish successful, self-fulfilled people from those who consistently fail to realize their goals. Standardized tests are the key parts of an assessment system that is meant to be central in determining whether a child will function successfully in the modern world as an adult. As such, they cannot succeed, because no such assessment system has ever been designed or used, nor is there any current theoretical basis for inventing such a system.

Instead, the exams just measure what every knowledgeable person said they would: the ability of children to take exams. They have spawned a whole new industry devoted exclusively to promoting successful performance on exams. All kinds of specialized books are published, based on past exams, focusing on the material most important to good performance. There are tutorial institutes, private coaches, remedial courses, and special preparatory courses (in elementary, middle, and high schools).

Special teacher-training seminars are devoted to helping teachers produce better results with their classes, because teacher pay and promotion are tied to those results. Administrators—principals, assistant principals, curriculum coordinators, school superintendents, and assistant superintendents—devote increasing proportions of their time and energy to improve their schools' grades, because their jobs are on the line.

It all comes back to one simple point: Exams do not assess anything significant to the future of children, because no one knows how to assess or measure the key factors to the future success of any person, child or adult. They are a closed system; tests exist for their own sake. They measure the ability of the entire school community—children, parents, teachers, administrators—to focus all their efforts on producing good results on tests! Nothing more, nothing less.

To say that such a massive effort, which basically turns the whole educational system on its head, is harmful is to seriously understate the case. The essential purpose of an educational system is to provide an environment that allows children to develop into successful adults. Replacing that with an educational system that forces children to perform well on a specific set of exams is nothing less than the end of schooling as a useful tool for society.

Perhaps the most devastating effect of standardized testing is the degradation of so many children who deviate from the testers' idea of the norm. Tests lead to singling out children and labeling them at the earliest possible age if, in the eyes of their teachers and testers, they do not seem to be able to fulfill all the requirements of the system in the required manner and time span. Tests form the basis for naming an unbelievably large group of children—more than one in five!—as somehow handicapped, a categorization that they carry with them throughout their lives. Tests subject children to the constant threat of punishment and to relentless criticism and virtually eliminate any free time from their lives. Tests rob most children of their childhood, strip them of their self-esteem, instill in them a lifelong distaste for anything academic, and create in them a well-deserved deep distrust of all adults.

Solving Problems

Problems are not objects of experience. They are abstractions extracted from experience by analysis. Reality consists of sets of interacting problems, which we refer to as "messes." Reality seldom consists of single isolated problems. Therefore, problems are to reality what atoms are to tables. We experience tables, not atoms. Because problems almost always exist as part of a set of problems, it is essential to be aware of the effects of the way we treat one of them on the others in the set. The failure to take such interactions into account led to a treatment of alcoholism in the 1920s (prohibition) as a separate problem. As a result, it had little effect on alcoholism but a big effect on organized crime. Taxing the value of property encourages its deterioration and conversion into tenements. Property taxes encourage the development of slums.

Exercises are abstracted from problems, themselves abstractions. The formulation of an exercise excludes the information required to formulate the underlying problem or, worse yet, the information required to solve it. For example, in a conversation with one of his colleagues, a university professor was asked how he would go about determining the probability that the next ball drawn from a bowl would be black if he knew the proportion and number of black balls that had previously been drawn and that the bowl contained only black and white balls. The professor said he would first ask how the one presenting the "problem" knew the bowl contained only black and white balls. The presenter said he did not have this information and that providing it would spoil the exercise. He was wrong; withholding that information had already spoiled the presentation of the problem.

An essential part of problem solving lies in determining what information is relevant in formulating it and in collecting that information. To deprive a student of the experience of specifying and seeking out such information is to miss most of the point of problem solving. Furthermore, it is usually harder to formulate the right problem correctly than to find the right solution after the problem has been properly formulated.

Exercises are purposeless problems. No motivation for solving them is provided to students other than getting an acceptable grade. Development of an ability to solve them gives students a false sense of security with respect to handling real problems in real situations.

A question is a still further abstraction from reality than an exercise. It is abstracted from an exercise. It eliminates the context in which an exercise arises. Contrary to the impression that the educational system promulgates, there are no absolute answers to questions; the correct answer to a question depends on the context in which it arises. For example, how much is 2 + 3? The answer depends on "two and three of what?" If we are speaking of 2 degrees Fahrenheit plus 3 degrees Celsius, the answer is different than if we are referring to the number of books on a table. How many students learn that 10 + 10 = 100 in a binary number system?

Schools are not only obsessed with the "one right answer" but also with the right questions. The American anthropologist Jules Henry made the point when he asked what would happen "if all through school the young were provoked to question the Ten Commandments, the sanctity of revealed religion, the foundations of patriotism, the profit motive, the two-party system, monogamy, the laws of incest, and so on."[10]

Ronald D. Laing, the eminent British psychiatrist, replied that there would be more creativity than society could currently handle, but not more than it should be capable of handling.[11] Keeping curiosity bottled up, as noted previously, is a "major preoccupation of institutions set up to manage the viable functioning of society." Thus, schools perform a societal function in suppressing an uncontrolled development of creativity. But if society is to be all it can be, even approximately, these institutions must liberate curiosity and not confine it autocratically.

Complex problem solving is natural to children; without that inborn ability, the human race would have long since perished. From the moment of birth, nearly every activity relates to a vast number of interrelated real-life problems that require solutions: How do I find food to satisfy my hunger? How do I keep warm? How do I create meaning out of the plethora of sensory inputs that assail me?

With each passing month, the number and complexity of the problems increase: locomotion, communication, orientation, and (above all and always) the ongoing meta-problem of making sense out of the world and out of our existence in it.

Children are masters at problem solving. Furthermore, as anyone knows who has ever closely observed a child in the process of learning how to crawl, or to walk, or to speak, children are persistent, committed problem solvers, adept at overcoming obstacles and imaginative in coming up with varied and often original solutions. Failure is met with resolve, unless continued application to the problem at hand is prevented by outside interference.

Schools, on the other hand, think that because all of life is basically about solving problems, children must be taught how to solve problems. Indeed, utilizing the curriculum as a vehicle to instill "techniques of problem solving" has become an important part of almost all pedagogical intercourse.

If the educational goal of teaching problem solving is in itself quixotic, the way schools go about it is, if anything, counterproductive. People in general muster their resources to solve real problems that confront them in the course of their lives; it is then, and only then, that they apply their experience to the matter at hand and seek assistance from others adept at the many-faceted art of problem solving.

In contrast, schools present a constant flow of artificial problems, regardless of whether they bear any relation to the issues that concern their client population. That children resist this and generally perform poorly in such an environment should come as no surprise. That schools greet their overall poor results by doing more of the same is just another example of doing the wrong thing with ever-increasing intensity. It is reminiscent of physicians not that long ago increasing the volume of bleeding their patients when the illness persisted—until the patients died; or of current medicine multiplying the number of antibiotics widely administered even in the face of growing evidence that this vastly increases the number of resistant bacteria available to create incurable epidemics.

If forcing students to apply themselves to artificial problems and exercises is a vain educational activity, doing educational and developmental research in artificial environments is even more damaging. Such research purports to uncover the way the human brain develops and functions. However, it takes places almost exclusively in what is termed "controlled situations," experimental environments constructed according to the preconceived notions and goals of the researcher. These environments, which are known to have a profound effect on the outcome of the experiments performed in them, are nevertheless taken to be representative of real-life situations that the studies purport to illuminate.

When applied to children, the situation is even more flawed than when applied to adults. Children tend to be less attuned to what adults want of them, and less easily diverted from their internally driven interests and goals. As a consequence of this well-known and easily observable fact, the results of laboratory studies done with children inevitably diverge widely from the way children behave and react in real-life conditions.

Ways of Treating Problems

There are four different ways to treat problems:

- Absolution
- Resolution
- Solution
- Dissolution, redesign

These form a hierarchy of effectiveness, from least to most. They are seldom made accessible to students in school. Below the university level, only two are ever used. In some curricula at the university level, three are exposed. The fourth and most effective way is rarely dealt with in the educational system, except in training for professions in which design is the principal process involved.

Absolution. Do nothing and let the problem solve itself or fade away. The problem is dealt with by default. When one's state of affairs is good and the environment is not changing, this way of dealing with problems is not bad. In a rapidly changing and turbulent environment, however, as ours is now, it can be disastrous. Problem absolution is like flying through a hurricane on automatic pilot. In such an environment, the only kind of equilibrium that can be obtained is dynamic.

Resolution. This involves returning to a previous state in one of two ways. In the first, one looks for a similar problem's occurrence in the past. What was done then? Did it work? If yes, it can be used again. If not, how can what was done be modified to be effective now? A second way to resolve a problem is to ask what has caused the problem, what is to blame for it? Then, if the cause or source of the problem is removed, one will be back where one was before the problem arose.

In systems thinking, blame becomes an obsolete concept. Problems are never the results of the actions of a single source, but of interactions of multiple sources. For example, it is apparent that the problems with education discussed here have no single source.

Resolution is an experiential way of treating problems based on qualitative judgments and common sense. It seeks treatments that are good enough, better than doing nothing but not necessarily the best that can be done. This is the way most everyday decisions are made, as well as those made less frequently.

Solution. To solve a problem is to use scientific methods, techniques, and tools to find the best that can be done, or the closest one can come to it. It uses quantitative techniques and often experimentation, in contrast to "raw" experience.

This way of dealing with problems was used extensively during World War II in the United Kingdom and came to be formalized in a discipline known either as operational research or management science. It spread rapidly thereafter and yielded a professional society and practitioners who are expert in the use of the procedures and tools developed. These tools are now widely taught and used at the university level in professional curricula. Before the university level, students are not likely to even hear of this development.

Following the development of formal methods of problem solving and the spread of their use, a surprising question began to be asked. Can one do better than the best that can be done? Is there a better way to deal with problems than solving them? There is, and it derives from two aspects of problem solving.

First, many problems that are solved do not stay solved because the context within which they were solved changes in fundamental ways. For example, the best way to travel between two cities when the weather is good might not be the best way to travel between them when there is a heavy snowstorm. Problem solutions often deteriorate under changing conditions. This is particularly apparent in the way we dress.

Second, every problem solution creates new problems and usually more than one and more difficult problems. For example, although Kepler solved the problems in Copernican astronomy, his solutions raised new problems in physics that weren't solved for decades, until Newton's work. Each solution found generated several new and more difficult problems. (Parents learn this when they buy one of their progeny their first automobile.) Scientific progress is due as much to the generation of new problems as to the generation of solutions to old ones. Is there a way to deal with problems that is less sensitive to environmental changes and that is not prone to produce new and more difficult problems? There is, and it involves *design*.

To *dissolve* a problem is to redesign the entity or system that has it, or its environment, so that it cannot arise again and is less likely to generate new problems.

Consider a very simple example. The paper book of matches that is usually provided when cigarettes, cigars, or pipe tobacco is purchased was the source of a serious problem a number of years ago. People would not close the book before striking a match on the abrasive at the bottom of the front of the package. Occasionally, a bit of the match's head would fly off and strike the other matches in the book. They would explode, thus burning the hand that held them. Printing at the bottom of the front of the book the words "Close cover before striking" had no significant effect on the number of burned hands, or of lawsuits against the producers.

Subsequently, manufacturers moved the abrasive on which the match was struck from the front to the back of the book, thus eliminating the possibility of creating a blaze that could burn a hand.

Except for practices that incorporate design as the way they practice—for example, architecture and engineering—the art of design is not incorporated into students' experiences in schools, despite its superiority in many situations, even to such analytical problem solving as scientists employ.

The power of design as an instrument of learning is almost completely overlooked by the educational system. For example, the best way to learn how an automobile (or any other mechanism) works and to gain understanding of why it works the way it does is to design one. Moreover, it is in design that people learn what they want. It is for this reason that customers are increasingly used to design stores and products that they use. For example, a group of men engaged in designing the men's store they wanted found that they wanted to group clothing by size, not type of clothing. They wanted one area, for example, where they could get any article of clothing they sought.

How much could be learned by allowing students to design the school they want, and the way they use it? A program at the University of Pennsylvania's Wharton School in Social System Sciences allowed students to design their own educational program, including the way they learned the subjects they wanted. Their design had to be presented and defended before a group of faculty who were practicing in the area the student wanted to enter. They could change their designs as they experienced them. These students left the college with the highest number of job offers and the highest average salaries of any of the college's graduates. Involving students in the design of their own school has been successful even at the K-12 level, in schools such as Sudbury Valley School in Framingham, Massachusetts.[12]

Before entering school, children learn at an incredible rate in the way they want to learn, not in a preprogrammed way. They manage on their own to convert their environments, however ill suited they are, into learning environments.

It is generally conceded that society is faced with the major problem of failing schools. In general, each of the four ways of treating problems has been applied to that one, too, and the result is worth reviewing.

Absolution. For more than a decade, from the end of World War II to the mid 1950s, nothing was done. The problem was expected to go away. Then Sputnik came, introducing just the kind of shocking, destabilizing change that puts everything into question. That put educators into high gear applying the second way.

Resolution. The tried-and-true way of improving schools was to modify the curriculum. In the past—for example, when the problem of absorbing huge masses of immigrants threatened to balkanize the country—this was done effectively by adding new material, such as social studies, civics, and more English language work. This model seemed to be tailor-made for the problem of the mid-twentieth century: What had to be done was to add more math and more science so that America could "keep up" with a world that seemed to be passing us by scientifically and technologically. (The fact that this turned out to be a myth is beside the point; at the time, the danger of falling behind seemed all too real.)

Another common way to improve schools was to upgrade and modernize the curriculum. This approach led to massively funded projects to rewrite most of the school curricula, under the leadership of college and university academics, who saw themselves as the carriers of the culture and, hence, best qualified to reform the way the culture is transmitted to children (this, despite the fact that few of them had any experience with young students).

Solution. Because technological research and development is quantitative, and depends on sophisticated testing and statistical analysis, these tools were imported into education beginning in the late 1980s and became the backbone of the "accountability" movement. Great emphasis was placed on scientific research in such fields as developmental and social psychology, cultural anthropology, neurology (especially brain function), economics, and indeed any field that could be dragged into the picture by means of a convincing grant proposal.

In fact, all of these attempts failed miserably. The first two foundered on their inapplicability to a wholly new cultural environment unlike any that had preceded this era; the third foundered on a gross overestimation of the degree to which researchers have unearthed any substantial understanding of human behavior.

This leaves *dissolution*, or redesign. The number of groups engaged in totally redesigning education in general, and schools in particular, is growing at an incredibly rapid pace, and there is a great deal to learn from them. It would seem that a high priority should be placed on giving the widest possible distribution to information about these redesign initiatives, and about their failures and successes.

It should be obvious that the best redesign is one in which the client population—the students—play a critical role. In fact, one is hard pressed to defend a process of redesign in which the client population for which the redesign is being performed is ignored. This is equally true in production and service organizations, where the clients are customers and consumers.

Creativity

Educational planners and designers do not seem to realize that solutions provided by students that satisfy teacher expectations cannot be creative. A creative solution or answer is one the recipients do *not* expect. A creative act always results in a surprise.

A creative act involves three steps. First, an assumption normally made in responding to a problem, exercise, or question, one that limits the number of alternative solutions or answers considered, is identified. Then, it is denied; the contradictory is assumed. Finally, the alternatives revealed by the contradictory assumption are then explored. This is a process that can be learned and developed with practice, but schools do not provide opportunities for doing so.

Puzzles and jokes are simple examples of creativity. A joke always has a surprise ending; an assumption the listener has made is denied, yielding a surprising conclusion to the story. A puzzle is a problem we can't solve because of something we incorrectly assume. The "trick" always lies in identifying the constraining assumption and denying it.

What one learns in school is that people in positions of authority expect answers and solutions with which they are familiar. They do not want to be surprised. For example, when my daughter was 13 years old, she was assigned the following "extra credit" problem in school. Nine dots forming a square were drawn on a sheet of paper (Figure 2.1). A handout instructed her to place a pen or a pencil on one of the dots and then draw four straight lines without lifting the pen or pencil from the paper—lines that would go through all nine dots. The usual solution to this puzzle requires going beyond the boundaries of the square (Figure 2.2). When she could not find a solution, she asked me for help. I explained that a puzzle is a problem you cannot solve because of something you incorrectly assume. Having said that, I proceeded to *fold* the paper (as shown in Figure 2.3) and, holding a felt-tip pen against the folded edge, produced two lines while drawing only one. Then, I unfolded the paper and easily covered the other dots with three lines (Figure 2.4).

●　　　●　　　●

●　　　●　　　●

●　　　●　　　●

Figure 2.1

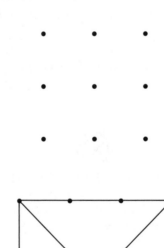

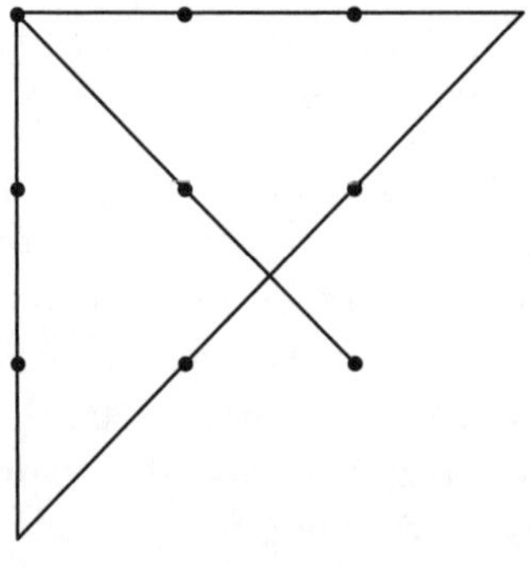

Figure 2.2

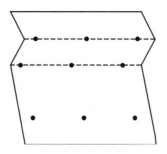

Figure 2.3

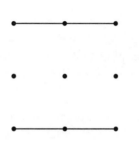

Figure 2.4

When my daughter presented this solution to her class, the teacher rejected it because she had folded the paper. She pointed out that the teacher's instructions had not prohibited it. The teacher said that nevertheless that was what she intended, and told my daughter to sit down. The fact is that there are a very large number of solutions to the puzzle, including ones that can do it with one line or even one dot! Keep in mind the instructions did not say how large a pen had to be used.

My daughter learned a very important lesson that day, one most of us learned in a similar way. The teacher was not interested in getting *a* solution to the puzzle, but to getting *the* solution she knew. The lesson learned in school then, is that when an authority asks a question, try to provide the answer the authority knows or expects. This lesson is carried through into corporations and other large organizations, where providing the bosses with the answer they want is standard operating procedure. This is why most people in positions of authority tend to convert their subordinates into clones.

That mass education was explicitly developed to mold naturally unruly children into compliant, obedient youngsters (and later, adults) is well documented.[13] Creativity was actively suppressed, and wholly unwelcome. Given the socioeconomic and political needs that these times require, the goal of mass education in the twenty-first century should be the fostering of every child's natural creativity, and the consequent development of an adult population that is inquisitive, original, and innovative.

It is generally not known that the suppression of creativity in schools extends even to the field of science, which is purportedly based on a foundation of free inquiry, of questioning every existing explanation of natural phenomena to constantly improve our understanding of how the world works. We are told repeatedly that what differentiates modern science from all natural philosophy that preceded it is its total lack of reliance on authority, and its absolute commitment to open-minded investigation.

Imagine, then, the reaction of students in schools when they encounter the science curriculum. In course after course, year after year, they are taught—and forced to memorize and regurgitate—the accepted dogmas of science as truths that are not to be challenged or questioned. This inconsistency is striking. Even more remarkable is what takes place in school laboratories, where students perform "scientific experiments."

Consider, for example, what happens in an introductory physics lab, when students do a simple experiment—for example, to determine the acceleration of gravity by rolling a ball down an incline and measuring how long it takes to reach the bottom. The protocol calls for repetition of the experiment and for some sort of statistical analysis of the results. Then, when students come up with their results, they discover that the results are "wrong!" Far from being praised for making a breakthrough discovery, they are informed that they have made a mistake because their answers do not conform to the accepted one. Needless to say, the students' understanding of what experimental science really is about cannot possibly be enhanced by such an approach, which unfortunately is ubiquitous in science classrooms. In all cases, the student is told what to look for, not asked to make an exploration that will ask real questions of nature.

3

Subjects and Disciplines

Nothing in education is so astonishing as the amount of ignorance it accumulates in the form of inert facts.

—Henry Brooks Adams

Compartmentalized Curricula

The subjects taught in the educational process are classified by disciplines. As a result, we are accustomed to thinking that problems are disciplinary by nature: for example, that there are physics problems, chemistry problems, biology problems, economics problems, psychology problems, and so on and on. There are absolutely no such things as disciplinary problems. The disciplinary description in front of the word *problem* tells us something, but nothing about the problem.[14]

To support this statement, we must show that problems are not disciplinary in nature and that there is considerable harm from assuming they are.

Consider the following example. An elderly woman in an inner-city neighborhood returned from a medical examination conducted at a free local clinic. It was the only medical facility to which she had access. On returning to her home, two rooms on the fourth floor of an old converted mansion, she had a heart attack and died. News of this was brought almost immediately to a meeting of university faculty members and community leaders. Because all present at the meeting knew the woman well, a depression settled over the meeting.

The first one to speak up was the professor of community medicine. He said, "I've been telling you we need more doctors in the clinic. We can't make house calls without them, and with them we might have prevented her death." No one commented. There was complete agreement.

After a pause, the professor of economics pointed out that there were plenty of doctors in the city but they were private practitioners whom she couldn't afford. He said, "What we need are either larger welfare payments so she could have afforded a doctor, or a national health-care plan that would have provided her with access to a private practitioner." Again, no comments followed.

The architect present then suggested that buildings of four floors or more that contained multiple dwelling units be required to provide elevators. Again, no comments.

Finally, the only woman present, a professor of social work, spoke up. "What a pity," she said, "you don't know anything about that woman. She was married as a teenager and shortly thereafter she gave birth to a son. She was simultaneously deserted by her husband whom she never saw again. She raised the son by doing menial housework, but with loving care. He was brilliant. On graduation from the public schools in his neighborhood, he competed for and won a Mayor's Scholarship to the University of Pennsylvania. He subsequently graduated at the top of his class and got a scholarship to the university's law school. Again, he was at the top of his class and was hired by the largest law firm in the city. He is now middle aged, a senior partner in the law firm. He is married with two children and lives in a beautiful house in one of the city's best suburbs. His house is all on one floor. If that woman had not been alienated from her son, she would have been living with him, where she would have had no steps to climb and all the money needed to call a doctor."

What kind of a problem was this? Medical, economic, architectural, or social work? None of these. The adjectives reveal the point of view of the person looking at the problem, not the nature of the problem. It is only by looking at a problem from many different perspectives that we can determine which one yields a way of treating it that provides the "biggest bang for the buck."

Because schools focus on separate disciplines, most adults classify problems by the location in which they arise or the discipline of the one who identified it. Then, they try to solve the problem using variables accessible to them. This is like a brain specialist trying to solve a headache by using brain surgery.

A classic story illustrates very well the potential cost of placing a problem in a disciplinary box. It involves a multistoried office building in New York. Occupants began complaining about the poor elevator service provided in the building. Waiting times for elevators at peak hours, they said, were excessively long. Several of the tenants threatened to break their leases and move out of the building because of this. The manager of the building then called for help from an engineering firm that specialized in elevator system design and operations.

The problem was described to the engineers, who then conducted a time study and determined that waiting times were excessive. They told management there were only three things that could be done to alleviate the situation. First, elevators could be added; second, the existing elevators could be replaced with faster ones; and finally, computer controls could be introduced with or without either of the two alternatives. This would send emptied elevators down to the ground floor when there was no one waiting for an elevator at a higher floor. Normally, the old elevators would go to the top of the building before returning to the ground floor.

Management authorized a study to determine what would be the best solution. The study revealed that because of the age of the building no engineering solution could be justified economically. The engineers said that management would just have to live with the problem permanently.

The desperate manager called a meeting of his staff, which included a young recently hired graduate in personnel psychology. The manager called for brainstorming in an effort to find a feasible solution to the problem. Despite the rules of brainstorming—positive suggestions only—each initial suggestion was beaten down by pointing out its deficiencies. The room went silent. The only one who had not participated in the discussion was the young personnel psychologist.

The general manager singled out the young man who had not yet spoken and asked whether he had an idea. The young man explained a reluctance to express it because of the negative attacks each suggestion had evoked. The manager dismissed his reason and instructed him to reveal his idea.

The young man had not focused on elevator performance but on the fact that people complained about waiting only a few minutes. Why, he asked himself, were they complaining about waiting for only a very short time? He concluded that the complaints were a consequence of boredom. Therefore, he took the problem to be one of giving those waiting something to occupy their time pleasantly. He suggested installing mirrors in the elevator boarding areas so that those waiting could look at each other or themselves without appearing to do so. The manager took up his suggestion. The installation of mirrors was made quickly and at a relatively low cost. The complaints about waiting stopped.

Today, mirrors in elevator lobbies and even on elevators in tall buildings are commonplace.

It has long been forgotten that the whole idea of dividing knowledge into separate distinct categories or disciplines originated with Aristotle, whose corpus consists of a series of textbooks defining the various fields he invented. Prior to Aristotle, this notion was never mentioned, as even a casual glance at Plato's dialogues would reveal. Aristotle's unquestionable brilliance and depth of understanding, not to mention unsurpassed wisdom, gave his way of looking at the world a primacy in Greek culture that was passed on, via Roman civilization, to Europe and its outposts, where it has remained one of the founding pillars of the Western worldview.

Whatever its merits in the past, this division of human experience into disciplines has long since been recognized as outmoded and even inimical to innovative insight. For some time, in the practical world of business and technology, people trained in specialized fields have been combined into "interdisciplinary teams," in an effort to mitigate the harmful influence that compartmentalized thought has on creativity and progress. Even academia, the last and most influential bastion of compartmentalized disciplines, has begun to show signs of flexibility in this regard. Courses and degree programs combining separate fields have slowly crept into the university world, albeit at a snail's pace.[15]

There is no longer the slightest justification for introducing children to the idea that human thought is a collection of fragmented "disciplines" and making that idea the center-pin of the educational experience for students in their schools. As a historical curio, this idea might make for an amusing aside in a general discussion of the evolution of human thought, but as a notion that is productive and useful for developing minds it is, at the very least, counterproductive. Children grow up seeing the world as a whole. Their greatest challenge—one that continues to be the central task of every person throughout life—is to form a worldview that makes sense out of the multitude of their experiences. Indeed, human sanity depends on the integrated nature of a person's worldview;

fragmented psyches are generally considered ill adapted to the needs of adult survival.

The educational environment of children should encourage them to continue to explore the open-ended connections between their experiences, and to be receptive to new interconnections and interpretations of theories and explanations that they have either learned or developed.

An oft-repeated story illustrates the deadening effect of thinking in terms of narrowly defined fields.[16] A high school physics student was given the following problem on an examination: "Suppose you were in a tall building, and had a sensitive barometer in your possession. How would you use it to find the height of the building?"

As anyone who has studied introductory physics will instantly recognize, the instructor was looking for the answer he had prepared his students to give—namely, measure the barometric pressure at the bottom and the top of the building, and calculate the height of the building, using the formula that relates the drop in barometric pressure to the increase in elevation going from the ground to the top of the building.

The student in question, a very bright and highly independent soul, found it demeaning to provide an answer that he thought was trivially easy. Instead, he answered, "You can do it several ways. One is to drop the barometer from the top of the building and measure how long it takes to hit the ground [thus illustrating that he knew the relationship between height, distance, and time in gravitational free fall, another piece of 'physics']. Another is to attach the barometer to a long string, lower it to the ground, and measure the length of the string [no longer 'physics,' but rather 'carpentry']."

The answer, of course, was declared wrong. The student objected strenuously and brought a storm of protest to bear on the examiner—who then agreed to repeat the same question and give the student an opportunity to provide the "correct" answer. The student, no more inclined to be compliant than before, answered, "I would go to the superintendent of the building and offer to give him the barometer as a gift if he would tell me how high his building is [now we have entered 'economics']."

Leaving aside the inanity of the original question, the story is a perfect illustration of the intellectual straitjacket that current schooling seeks to impose on imaginative young minds. In corporations, the equivalents of disciplines in colleges and universities are functions (for example, production, marketing, and finance), product classes, or market-defined units. There are no such things as production or marketing problems, but there are problems that are erroneously treated as thought they were.

Science and Humanities

The disciplinary distinction that probably does most harm is between science and the humanities. This is a distinction crystallized by Charles Snow in his famous lecture, "The Two Cultures."[17] He described them as in opposition to each other. The educational system tends to reinforce this characterization. The fact is that science and the humanities are two sides of the same coin, different aspects of the same thing. They can be viewed separately, but they cannot be separated.

The humanities (including the arts) are concerned with finding differences among things that are apparently similar. Autobiographies and novels are about different lives or different views of the same life. They focus on the uniqueness of their subjects and events, as do histories and linguistic studies. Great art is the product of distinctive points of view. The difference between portrayals of the same subject by different artists lies in the way they looked at their subject, not their subject matter. Great artists who have painted the same subject many times (for instance, Rembrandt's self- portraits) have done so differently each time, and each is unique.

Biography and autobiography focus on the uniqueness of their subject. A psychologist working on the same individual looks for generalities that can be used to explain the subject's unique characteristics.

Science (including its derivative, technology) is concerned with finding similarities among things that are apparently different. The similarities are expressed in laws and theories. The humanities reveal the problems yet to be solved. Science and technology try to solve these problems by developing general principles or methodologies that apply to them.

This is not to say that humanists do not try to solve problems or that scientists do not try to formulate them. However, their approaches to formulating and solving them differ. Humanists are inclined to solve problems experientially and qualitatively, by resolving them. Scientists are inclined to solve problems experimentally and quantitatively. Systems thinkers, who deny the possibility of separating science and the humanities, are partial to problem dissolving. It is impossible for humanists not to use some of the output of science, and it is equally impossible for scientists not to use some of the output of humanists.

Actually, one of the best kept secrets of our time is that the distinction between science and art is wholly nonexistent. In fact, the single most significant development that differentiates modern science from earlier science is that, beginning about 500 years ago in western Europe, the fundamental barrier between science and art was removed. Prior to this daring act, science was firmly associated with common sense and hard, practical experience, whereas art was equally firmly associated with fantasy and imagination. Modern science was born when natural philosophers (as scientists were called in those days, and until recently) cast off their aversion to fantasy and imagination and embraced these two aspects of human thought as integral to an understanding of the natural world.

Every significant development in modern science can be traced directly to a fantasy that defies common sense and seems absurd, even now, to people with two feet planted firmly on the ground. The list is endless: Copernicus's notion that the Earth hurtles through space and spins on its axis; Galileo's ideas that heavy bodies and light bodies fall at the same rate, that bodies can move without any force being exerted on them, and that the moon is made of rock; Kepler's insistence that the planets (including the Earth) move in ellipses rather than circles; Newton's musings that any two pieces of matter in the universe are attracted to each other by a force that acts across any distance without a material connection between the two; Maxwell's description of all of space filled with an undetectable "aether," which carries electric and magnetic vibrations everywhere; Planck's suggestion that energy comes in little packets; Schrodinger's, that matter consists of packets of waves; Einstein's, that all space is curved and inextricably linked with time.

When Galileo pointed his telescope at the moon and declared that it contained mountains and oceans, he was considered utterly insane. The Catholic Church, long the champion of the best scientific work being done in Europe, was doing humanity a favor by attempting to curb the influence of such ranting! How could a rock stay up in the sky? How could any sensible conclusion be drawn from an instrument that contained not one, but two, objects called "lenses," which were known to distort the way things actually looked!

The mark of a creative scientist, whatever aspect of the natural world the scientist is studying, is the extent to which he or she can combine hard, verifiable experience with imaginative explanations. It is the artistry in science that makes it vulnerable to great debates among its leading lights—people who form vastly different pictures of what the world is like, all in the name of explaining its workings.[18]

Needs Not Known

Educators and educational planners spend a great deal of time deciding what subjects students should be taught. (Taught, not learned!) Such is the nature of "curricular design." This activity clearly assumes that those making these decisions know what students will need to know when they leave school. This assumption is generally false for two reasons.

First, a great deal of what adults must know to do their jobs after finishing school is developed after they have finished school. Recall from Chapter 1, "Learning and Teaching," the incident in which I realized that, in the past 50 years, I had not taught a course on a subject that existed when I was a student, and that everything I learned I mastered without it being taught to me. New technology and new information, knowledge, and understanding are continuously becoming available. Curricular planners cannot anticipate all these developments. Because computers were not yet available when we, the authors, were in grade school, there were no courses on their use. Nevertheless, most in our generations can use computers today. This is why the most important thing for students to learn is how to learn and to be motivated to do so throughout their lives.

As knowledge accumulates, more and more formal education is offered to those who want to work "at the frontiers." Refresher courses of many types and duration have become commonplace. As the rate of acquisition of knowledge and understanding continues to accelerate, and it will, education will increasingly be extended and come to be thought of as continuous over a lifetime. This makes the separation of work, play, and learning less and less tenable.

During the Industrial Revolution, activities were taken apart and reduced to the smallest groupings that could be dealt with separately. Work, play, and learning were separated and housed in completely separate institutions and facilities. Factories were designed for work; play and learning were excluded. Country clubs and ballparks, for example, were designed for play, excluding work and learning. Schools were designed for teaching, excluding play (except for short recesses) and work. Because work, play, and learning are increasingly seen as different aspects of the same thing, the distinction between the three types of institutions becomes blurred. This has already begun in the workplace. An increasing number of employers provide facilities for each type of activity. However, schools, with only rare exceptions, have remained immune to this development.

Indeed, another way of describing the era in which we live is as a time when the rate of innovation and change far exceeds that of any preceding era. This means that new developments will change the nature of virtually every aspect of our lives at a dizzying clip, new worlds inexorably replacing existing worlds repeatedly within the span of a single lifetime.

The authors' lives encompass the last half of the twentieth century. We remember well a world before refrigerators, before supermarkets and shopping malls, before electronic fund transfers, before television and teleconferencing, before computers, before jet planes and GPS systems and CDs and DVDs and direct long-distance dialing and solar power and nuclear energy or weapons and quantum field theory and …. There is no way to begin to describe the transformation in dry sentences.

Children today inhabit a world that makes ours appear to have moved at a snail's pace. Can it really be that, as late as the mid-1990s, the Internet was barely a factor in human affairs, and web pages were exotica?

To people trained in traditional schools, all this seems perplexing and upsetting. The anxiety that permeates the world of adults is palpable; their world is transforming itself constantly, and they feel at a loss at how to orient themselves in this ever-shifting environment—all because the fundamental message conveyed to today's adults when they were children, during years of schooling that were allegedly preparing them for life in the modern world, was that the curriculum of their schools provided an adequate framework for the world of their future, today's world—but it didn't!

In fact, however, nature has provided every child with the key tool for becoming fully adept at finding his or her way in a world of rapid change. A moment's reflection will reveal that this must be so, because the world of infants and young children is, and always has been, one of frighteningly rapid change, even during all those millennia in which the world of adults has not been. To a child, the overwhelming majority of impressions and experiences encountered from day to day are new, unexpected, and incomprehensible. Without the innate ability to maneuver in such a world, and to make sense of it somehow, no child would survive.

The magical tool provided by nature is play. All children know how to play from birth. Play is nothing other than an activity—any activity—that takes place without a known endpoint or goal. Whether the play involves open-ended, random exploration—such as that engaged in by a philosopher "playing with" a new idea or by a child playing with sticks—or whether the play involves preset rules that enable you to advance from one point to another—such as that engaged in by children playing soccer or by a poet developing a sonnet—in all cases, the protagonist is exploring the unknown. Children do this with gusto, without fear, and with confidence in their ability to deal with whatever outcome they encounter.

In addition, play is an activity that brings joy and satisfaction just from engaging in it, for its own sake.

The very raison d'être of educational institutions at all levels should be to provide an environment in which some form of play predominates, where play is understood in its broadest sense of free exploration, supported and encouraged by educators. Children growing up in such an environment would be equipped, as adults, to deal with the unknown future as competently as they could when they were young.[19] Adults placed in such an environment would be helped to shed the unexamined routines and assumptions that they have accumulated over time.

4

The New World

True education makes for inequality: the inequality of individuality, the inequality of success, the glorious inequality of talent, of genius. For inequality, not mediocrity, individual superiority, not standardization, is the measure of the progress of the world.

—Felix E. Schelling

The Old World

The Industrial Revolution was about the mechanization of work, the replacement of man by machine as a source of energy. Machines replaced people's muscles. Work was defined as a change in one or more properties of matter by the application of energy to it. For example, moving an object, boiling water, converting iron ore to iron, forging iron and making paper out of wood pulp all involve physical work. The machine became the emblem of this revolution. The factory in which machines produced goods became the principal product of the new age. And schools were designed to be like factories.

As we have discussed earlier, from an educational point of view, the old era was ushered in by the Industrial Revolution and, therefore, is widely identified as the industrial age. This revolution created a serious problem for society. Mechanized production required people to act as though they were parts of a machine. Normal people actually do not want jobs that force them to behave like parts of machines. It was the work of people like Frederick Taylor that forced designers of mechanized production to employ and use people as though they were replaceable machine

---

parts.[20] Machine-like work was necessary to produce a flourishing industrial economy. How did Western society go about creating millions of people who were willing to act like automatons, doing simple tasks repetitively so that they and others could enjoy a higher standard of living?

The solution lay in public education. Such education was designed to take control of children—not those of the elite, but of the masses—to teach them the kinds of behavior and rudimentary skills they needed to work in the industrial era. And chief among these new skills is the wholly unnatural one of being able to function as a part of a machine. This was a tall order.

Two things were required to fill the order. First, school had to break the free spirit of children. It had and has to force them to want to sit still in one place, get in lines, be quiet, and do what they are told to do—no more running around having fun. No more doing what they wanted to do, no more unconstrained following of their curiosity—instead, acceptance of strict discipline. All children who entered school had and have to do the same thing at the same time. They were and are punished if they didn't conform.

Second, school had to teach them specific skills that would enable them to work effectively in mechanized factories. These were identified as "the three Rs": reading, writing and 'rithmetic. School had to teach them to read, because they must be able to read instructions. It had to teach them to write so that they could do required paperwork. It had to teach them arithmetic so that they were comfortable with weights and measures, and so that they could and can do the standard bookkeeping required in the industrial economy both for themselves and for their employers. The three R's are, in short, the three basic industrial skills required to carry out the Industrial Revolution, and they formed the heart of the curriculum used by schools.

Schools were designed to be industrialized disseminators of information and instruction using materials and methods that were appropriate when students capable of working in factories were taken to be their desired output. The educational system treated students as black boxes whose output would hopefully exactly match what was put into them. Pavlov's concept of the use of reward and punishment to reinforce learning permeated design of pedagogy.[21]

As pointed out earlier, the educational system expects students to be able to do what can be done better by computers, tape recorders, and cameras. Students know this and resent it, even if only unconsciously. Computers can remember more and recall, compare, and calculate more quickly and accurately than students can.

Contrary to what schools do, what is most important for students to learn is what computers and other electronic devices cannot do. Furthermore, teachers forget that forgetting what is irrelevant is one of our most important abilities.

The educational system treats students as a product to be worked on and put together on an assembly line, scheduled processes in which they are passed from one operation to another. The processing itself is increasingly done by machines (for example, in grading papers and producing class schedules and assignments). In short, today's schools are modeled after factories. The incoming student is treated like raw material coming onto a production line that converts them into finished products. Few concessions are made to the animated state of the students. They are lined up alphabetically, marched in step, silenced unless spoken to, seated in rows, periodically inspected and examined, and so on. The material worked on varies widely, but their treatment is uniform. The system tries to minimize the variety of outputs it produces. The educational process is considered to be successful if the finished product can be sold at a high price.

Industrial cultures have as their guiding model a mechanized worldview. Just as the universe is seen as a giant machine, ordered by undeviating rules of motion, so too industrial cultures, based on the beneficent plenitude provided by machines, seek a social organization governed by undeviating, orderly rules. Historically, industrial societies have, therefore, all developed methods to ensure the survival of their industrial lifestyle; first, during childhood and second, throughout adult life.

The primary industrial survival mechanism is overt control of the individual by the community. Indeed, one of the distinguishing features of industrial cultures is strong central governance, ranging from monarchs claiming divine authority to democratically elected rulers, all supported by police and armies.

To control children, schools were established to channel the development of children in a manner demanded by the culture. These schools fulfill their cultural purpose as follows:

- Schools "keep children off the streets." In other words, they physically incarcerate children during their formative years for much of the day.

- Schools expose children constantly to the culture's values, through the agency of adult *teachers*. The most important virtue a teacher must possess is loyalty to the culture's value system. Everything else is secondary. This is the foundation of all teacher training and teacher selection in every industrial society.

  Cries for changes in teacher training or teacher qualification carefully skirt this point; in fact, the essential nature of teacher training has changed little over time, as has the nature of teaching as a profession. This is the way industrial cultures want it to be. Thus, the teacher as master of a field of knowledge is *not* what the schools want at all, because masters tend to be independent, have their own approaches and ideas, and may even lead to change. It is important, by contrast, that teachers have only a casual acquaintance with any field so that they can, at best, grasp and transmit the currently accepted version of the subject matter and not challenge or embellish it. Similarly, the social status of teachers is carefully kept in the middle of the spectrum—high enough to command some respect, especially among the masses of industrial workers but not high enough to attract truly creative or dynamic or imaginative people to the profession, at least not routinely.

- Schools channel children's energy toward the acquisition of the skills needed in an industrial economy.[22] In the United States, there has been a never-ending stream of curriculum reassessments, more frantic in recent years as the country slips out of the industrial lifestyle while the educational establishment strains to treat it as still an industrial culture.

  After the assessment has been made, the school curriculum is created to reflect those needs, and the flow of children into the various skill groups is regulated by overseers chosen by the culture for this purpose. The chief overseers in this country are the various groups and agencies, both governmental and private, that parcel out funds for the support of teacher training, student scholarships, materials, and promotion in the particular fields chosen for attention.

One important tool in the process of overseeing the flow of students into particular disciplines has been forced exposure of youngsters to a chosen spectrum of disciplines, and a subsequent weeding-out process, done through a variety of tests and evaluations, to help the overseers make choices in the channeling process. As the selection process becomes more complex in an ever-more-complex industrial setting, the tests become more frequent, more comprehensive, and more controlling: The greater fine-tuning required in a complex economy invites more intervention and control.

As an industrial culture grows older and becomes more intricate, the curriculum and the control mechanisms also gain in intricacy. There is an inexorable drive, as time passes, to add more subjects to the list being offered in schools, as the industrial technology branches out to encompass a wider range of control over the physical environment. A glance at recent curriculum guides for ages K-12 issued by the federal Department of Education, and by the education departments of the various state authorities, reveals a growing tendency to include in the universal curriculum the full range of human knowledge. In fact, there isn't the faintest hope for any single individual to accumulate a meaningful overview of human knowledge today; and the wider the domain of knowledge any person seeks to gain, the more superficial will that person's mastery of that knowledge be. Furthermore, the extent of information available now is so great that any attempt to identify this or that part of it as more important, or more significant, than any other is shortsighted and runs counter to the unfailing historical experience that each generation finds its most significant information in precisely those areas that were given short shrift by earlier generations.

As Colin Cherry put it:

> Leibnitz, it has sometimes been said, was the last man to know everything. Though this is most certainly a gross exaggeration, it is an epigram with considerable point. For it is true that up to the last years of the eighteenth century our greatest mentors were able not only to compass the whole science of their day, perhaps together with mastery of several languages, but to absorb a broad culture as well. But as the fruits of scientific labor have increasingly been applied to our material betterment, fields

of specialized interest have come to be cultivated and the activities of an ever-increasing body of scientific workers have diverged. Today we are most of us content to carry out an intense cultivation of our own little scientific gardens (to continue the metaphor), deriving occasional pleasure from a chat with our neighbors over the fence, while with them we discuss, criticize, and exhibit our produce.[23]

Even critics of the industrial educational system concede that it does its job well, albeit at an exorbitant human price. As Jonathan Kozol has noted: "U.S. education is by no means an inept, disordered misconstruction. It is an ice-cold and superb machine. It does the job: not mine, not yours, perhaps, but that for which it was originally conceived.... The first goal and primary function of the U.S. public school is not to educate good people, but good citizens.... In the double talk of Schools of Education, we employ...elegant expressions like 'the socializing function.' The function is...: 12 years of mandatory self-dehumanization, self-debilitation, blood loss."[24]

The essential nature of the learning process is strongly interfered with in industrial cultures. The dominant form of learning, encouraged through rewards and punishments, is instruction in skills. Learning through exploration, and through other self-motivated activities, is severely curtailed in a variety of ways. The very act of incarceration of children in schools severely limits their access to their surroundings. In addition, forays into physical or intellectual territories not approved by the official curriculum are severely repressed through disapproval, rejection, penalties, and frequently social ostracism (enforced isolation, commitment to mental institutions, imprisonment).

In the industrial educational system, the right subject must be mastered in the right way at the right time. Thus, children are not supposed to be taught a particular field "too early" (especially not by someone like a parent, outside the approved educational system) or "too late" (which makes them slow learners, retarded in their acceptable rate of progress). The books for instruction are carefully selected and monitored; authorities choose them, and publishers adhere to the approved formulas at the risk of losing their money on an unmarketable text. School libraries are carefully screened and little used except on approved projects. The entire field of developmental psychology and educational psychology is constructed, using industrial-style scientification, to encourage the notion that mechanized, uniform treatment of children in the schools is justifiable and based on proper scientific evidence. There is little point in entering into a debate with these industrial-age theoreticians; their existence is needed to justify the measures taken by an industrial culture to perpetuate its lifestyle.

Authoritarian governments have long used confinement to psychiatric institutions and ostracism through psychiatric treatment and labeling as weapons to control citizens. What is not generally recognized is the extent to which *all* industrial cultures use these weapons to keep their entire population, including children, restricted to well-defined, acceptable modes of public behavior. In sharp contrast to pre-industrial cultures, which find ways to integrate into their fabric persons exhibiting any and every mode of behavior (including those we would label as severely psychotic), industrial cultures, if they are to maintain the regimentation required in an industrial economy, must suppress behavior that lies outside the range of prescribed norms. Mavericks everywhere are cast out of the flow of life, and this process begins—as one would expect—in childhood, in the schools, the better to impress the growing individual with the need to adhere to proper behavior patterns throughout adult life. The "better" the industrial school system, the more intensely it monitors "aberrant" behavior, through psychologists, specialists, and wholly or partially segregated facilities, manned lavishly and supported extravagantly by public funds. Difficulties children have in dealing with the official curriculum often come to be labeled as mental or behavioral disorders, subject to professional "treatment."

The question is never "Why do people behave like sheep, like followers, in an advanced industrial culture?" There is no question, because the need for such behavior is at the heart of industrial society's ability to survive. If anything, the question is, "How do innovators ever survive in an industrial culture?" and the answer is that it is a statistical quirk, an oddity that crept in through the cracks, because the overwhelming majority of innovators, even those who ultimately become heroes after their time, *don't* survive!

Industrial cultures bear within them the seeds of perpetual intracultural warfare, caused by the tensions created by the control mechanisms industrial cultures must employ to bend human nature to the needs of the industrial machines. Human beings, by nature free agents, by nature roving explorers, by nature self-movers, by nature freewheeling model builders, resist at every available level the efforts of an industrial culture to restrict their activities to the range permitted by the culture. This built-in conflict between human nature and the nature of the industrial lifestyle produces a wide range of disruptive psychosocial phenomena that are universal in all industrial cultures and threaten always to tear them apart from within.

In the realm of education, these tensions manifest themselves in widespread resistance to learning within the schools. As Gilbert Highet put it, "Why is teaching often so difficult for teachers? And why is learning nearly always so hard for the pupils? There are many reasons; but one certainty is that, as most schools are set up today in the Western world, learning is something compulsory. It is an Ought: even worse, a Must. And in the lands of freedom the young now sneer at the Oughts and evade or resist the Musts with all their energy."[25]

The New World

We have all grown so jaded by the constant proclamations of new eras and new beginnings that we seem to have trouble recognizing the real thing when it finally arrives. But the new era is indeed at hand, and the old is fading and fraying with remarkable speed.[26]

—Leslie Gelb

Although awareness of the new era is spreading, there has yet to be consensus on its essential characteristics and the name by which it should be known. Some have referred to it as the Post-Industrial Revolution, or the information age, or the age of uncertainty, or the age of Gaia, or the age of heretics, or the new capitalism, or the network society, or the age of access. It is too early to expect agreement on a name. After all, it took several hundred years before the Western world settled on the name Renaissance. However it is labeled, awareness of the nature of the new era and the transformations that are producing it are not being responded to by most schools, by most institutions of "higher learning," or by most continuing-education programs designed for professionals and laymen.

The transformation of the Industrial Revolution into the Post-Industrial Revolution gives rise to a very different concept of schooling and learning.

This new revolution is based on the emergence of three technologies in the nineteenth century that came into their own in the twentieth century. First, there was the telegraph, a device that did not do physical work but which *transmitted* symbols; it mechanized *communication*. It was followed, of course, by a sequence of important improvements such as the telephone, radio, and television.

The second technological development was radar and sonar, which were instruments that *observed and generated* symbols that constitute data. These, too, did no work in the physical sense. They were also followed by much more sophisticated devices—for example, the electron microscope, X-rays, ultrasound, and MRIs.

Finally, there was the computer, which *logically manipulated* symbols. This, too, was not physical work. John Dewey called such treatment of symbols "thinking."[27] For this reason, the computer was called a "thinking machine."

When these three technologies are brought together, they generate data, process it into information and knowledge, and transmit these to places that need them. These are *mental* functions; they are instruments that replace some of the functions of man's mind. This has come to be called *automation*, which is to the Post-Industrial Revolution what mechanization was to the first. It is not a mere extension of the Industrial Revolution, but a fundamental difference in kind.

When schools were thought of as factories, they were designed to facilitate teaching, not learning. In general, architects and educators have yet to try to design educational environments intended to facilitate learning rather than teaching. Those few schools (such as the Sudbury Valley School in Framingham, Massachusetts) that are built around learning have had to adapt buildings built for other purposes. But, the ways in which they differ from conventional schools provide clues as to what institutions designed for learning would look like. Keep in mind that most learning is done at home, at work, or outdoors.

Another aspect of current school design is a major deficiency: Schools are in use a very small proportion of the time because they are designed for only one function. For most of a day's 24 hours, they are unoccupied. For many weeks of the year, they are not in use. This suggests that there are other related uses to which school buildings could be put if they were designed for multiple functions, the presence of which could augment the educational process. Schools should act as community centers, as locations for adult education, and as centers for provision of government services. Schools might well be combined with public libraries and buildings that house public services such as the local government and police. Students could learn a great deal through exposure to the activities in such buildings. It would also do a great deal to integrate learning into other normal activities.

Finally, it should be noted that schools—especially colleges and universities—have faculty offices that are designed and arranged like cells in a monastery. They reveal eloquently the hypocrisy of claims of educators that they seek interdisciplinarity in education. Separation of faculty members in the same discipline by spaces that are not directly connected to each other, and faculty members of different disciplines in different buildings or different floors of buildings, furthers the isolation and inaccessibility of faculty.

Although the post-industrial lifestyle is still in the early stages of emergence, it is possible to detect some of its chief characteristics at this stage of its development.

Perhaps most striking is the fact that the technology of communications creates, in effect, a *global mind* in which each individual can participate. By a global mind, I mean a universal repository in which all events are recorded as they occur; everything that has been recorded is stored in an appropriate fashion in a global memory; and everything stored is accessible in whatever form the accessors wish to have and can be manipulated in any way they want. The present and the past, on a cosmic scale, are all integrated into a great reservoir of experience that can be analyzed and studied at will.

Together with the new communications technology, the new technology of transportation turns the world into a single village, in the true sense of the term—namely, the movement of persons and goods from one spot to another globally is less difficult (in time, energy, and expense) than the movement of persons and goods was in pre-industrial times from village to village.

In addition, the post-industrial era holds out the promise that the economy of production will ultimately virtually free humanity from concern for survival. The production of material goods needed for basic human existence will increasingly be carried out through routinized procedures that, *like all routinized procedures,* will approach complete automation. The bulk of people's time, effort, and economic activity will tend more and more toward the creation of nonessential products designed according to the value scheme of the particular culture engaging in the activity.

It is already evident that the post-industrial lifestyle, regardless of the culture that embraces it, places high value on such traits as *creativity, originality, aesthetic satisfaction, beauty, understanding, insight, curiosity, scholarliness,* and *wisdom.* The post-industrial society is a fertile garden for the flourishing of the human spirit, in harmony with itself. The post-industrial human soul is primarily engaged in the perpetual, internally driven wrestling to reveal new secrets, create new patterns, and conquer new worlds of the mind.

All of these fundamental transformations have changed the landscape of education radically.

The Thinking Revolution

Albert Einstein once said, "We can't solve problems by using the same kind of thinking we used when we created them." The current educational system fails to make students aware of what the current pattern of thought is, of what problems are facing us that it does not enable them to deal with successfully, and of what new pattern of thought does enable them to do so.

In the Western world, after the Renaissance, following Descartes and Newton, the universe was generally believed to be a mechanism that was created by God to do his work. It was also believed that it could be known and understood completely by use of a way of thinking called "analysis."

Analysis is a three-step pattern of thought that comes naturally to us. It can be seen in the way most children try to gain understanding of something—like a toy or radio—that they do not understand:

1. The thing to be known or understood is taken apart.

2. The behavior or properties of the parts taken separately are described or explained.

3. And, the descriptions and explanations of the parts are aggregated into knowledge or an alleged "understanding" of the whole, the thing to be explained.

For example, when asked to describe or explain a university, we begin by breaking it down into colleges. Then we go to departments, and then to curricula, followed by courses and classes, the organizational elements. Then we identify the indivisible parts of which a university is made up: students, faculty, administration, and support personnel. We describe what each does that contributes to the functioning of the whole, and then aggregate this into an attempt to explain the nature of the whole, the university.

After World War II, with the growth of interest in the nature of "systems," it became apparent that the behavior and properties of systems could not be understood by analyzing them. A different way of thinking was required. To understand this development, we must first know what a system is.

A system is a whole that is defined by its function in a larger system of which it is a part.

For example, the telephone system is defined by its function: the transmission of voice from one person to another.

Every system contains at least two essential parts, parts without which it cannot perform its defining function.

For example, an automobile's motor and transmission are necessary for performance of its function; its windshield wipers and ashtrays are not.

A system's essential parts satisfy three conditions:

1. *Each can affect the behavior or properties of the whole.*

2. *The way they affect the whole depends on what at least one other part is doing. (In other words, the effects of the parts are interdependent.)*

3. *Subsets of the essential parts (subsystems) can also affect the behavior and properties of the whole, but none has an independent effect on the whole.*

It follows from the nature of a system that when it is taken apart it loses all of its defining properties. (A disassembled automobile cannot carry anyone anywhere. A disassembled computer cannot compute.) When a system is analyzed, it is first taken apart, but it loses all its defining properties when this is done. Therefore, *a system cannot be understood by analyzing it.* Its behavior and properties cannot be explained by analyzing it. For example, no amount of analysis of British automobiles will explain why they drive on the left rather than the right as we do. No amount of analysis will explain why we use Arabic rather than Roman numerals.

Analysis of a system reveals *how it works;* it provides know-how, knowledge, not understanding; that is, explanations of why it works the way it does. This requires *synthetic thinking.* This is also a three-step process, each of which is the opposite of the corresponding step in analysis. In the first step of synthesis, the system to be explained is identified as a part of (contained in) a larger system. (For example, an automobile is part of the transportation system; a university is part of the educational system.)

In the second step, the function of the containing system is then explained. (What is the function of the transportation system, the educational system? Transportation: a way of intentionally moving things from one place to another. Education: a way of enabling people to develop into and maintain and sustain themselves as effective adults, to enjoy themselves in the process, and to contribute to the development of the communities of which they are a part and others within them.)

Finally, the system in question is explained by disaggregating the containing system and identifying the function of the system in question within the system that contains it. (The automobile is designed to move people at will from a starting point of their choice to an ending point of their choice, in privacy, and on land. For a long time, it was designed to carry six passengers because it was intended for use by the average American family, then numbering 5.6. It is getting smaller because the average family now numbers about 3.2.)

Note that analysis begins by taking things apart and yields knowledge. Synthesis begins by putting things together and yields understanding. Analysis is the way scientists conduct research. Synthetic thinking is exemplified in *design.* The current educational system fails to make students aware of these different patterns of thought and what each can and cannot do.

There is one other extremely important aspect of synthetic thinking. The systems with which we deal are becoming increasingly complex. Think, for example, of the difference between a neighborhood grocery store and a global chain of retail stores like Wal-Mart or the difference between a tent or shack and a skyscraper. Scientists are searching for a way of dealing effectively with such complexity. Unfortunately, most of them are approaching the subject analytically. The result is identification of such a large number of variables and relationships between them that we are not able to handle them. However, if complexity is approached synthetically, by design, as in the design of a skyscraper or a city, there seems to be no limit to the complexity we can handle effectively.

It is not so much that synthetic thinking is absent from the school curriculum, as that analytic thinking dominates it.

Synthetic thinking is the normal way human beings think about things. From earliest infancy, the world impinges on us as a whole, and we each have to learn to deal with the lifelong task of making it meaningful and sensible for ourselves.

Analytic thinking was introduced as a possibly useful tool by the scientists of the early modern age. Overwhelmed by the complexity of the cosmos, they sought ways to break it up in the hope that the pieces would be simpler to deal with. The more sophisticated of them understood that this was, at best, a mechanism for sorting our impressions of reality into components that might yield us some new insights into the functioning of the whole.

Thus, for example, physicists could focus on the gravitational attraction between two bodies, even though two bodies never existed apart from the rest of the universe, and the behavior ascribed to two bodies acting on each other never corresponded to the behavior of any real bodies in the world. Even the analytic division of interactions between material bodies into gravitational, electrical, magnetic, and other forces could only serve as a guide to potential insights into the behavior of actual material systems, none of which ever displayed interactions of only one type.

Creative and original physicists understood this and always sought for more integrated ways of understanding the universe. The surprising degree of usefulness of their analytic methods did not distract the more profound thinkers among them from searching for a comprehensive, synthetic understanding of physical phenomena—a search that will doubtless go on until the end of time, as new ways of viewing the whole of human experience continue to emerge.

Education is permeated by expositions of analytic thinking. This begins with simplistic presentations of scientific material—that is, material related to the functioning of the physical world—and flows over into presentations of almost all areas of intellectual endeavor, even those least amenable to such an approach. Even as the leading edge of current attempts to explain the workings of nature and the mysteries of human affairs moves away from analysis and toward the more synthetic approach that is natural to human thought, our educational system hangs on to outmoded ways of thought.

The situation would be greatly improved in an educational system that granted freedom to all students, of every age, to follow their own unique path toward understanding, and to seek on their own initiative the intellectual tools they find most congenial to help them along that path. For those seeking to deepen their understanding of their environment, there is little reason to doubt that mastering different patterns of thought will be at the top of their priorities.

5

Antidemocratic Schooling

There is, I think, no point in the philosophy of progressive education which is sounder than its emphasis upon the importance of the participation of the learner in the formation of the purposes which direct his activities in the learning process, just as there is no defect in traditional education greater than its failure to secure the active cooperation of the pupil in construction of the purposes involved in his studying.

—John Dewey

There are three root ideas underlying the ethical, political, and social structure of the United States. These three ideas serve as guiding principles for the nation as a whole. They are, in a sense, overarching ideals toward which we strive. There is no denying that the American people have fallen short of converting these ideas into practical reality; but, the ideas nevertheless remain, clear and sharp, as our basic underpinning, and our failures to live by them have spurred us to work toward their full realization.

The first of these is the idea of individual rights: Every person is endowed with certain "inalienable rights," rights that belong to people as their own, as their inherent possession—not granted as a gift by some benevolent ruler, not given as a privilege by an all-powerful state, but belonging to them, without qualification, as their rights.

It is not necessary to agree on the source of these rights. Some people hold that they emanate from God. Other people think that they derive from some natural law governing man. Still others think they are rooted in a science of man and society. There are many philosophical theories about the rights of man—and many people who have no theory whatsoever believe in them intuitively. All agree that inviolate individual rights exist and are essential to our way of life.

It is also not necessary to agree on the exact number and nature of these rights. Different people, different communities, and different times have somewhat different lists. For example, the right of privacy is only now gradually coming into its own. By contrast, the right of free speech is high on everyone's list and has been from the beginning of our history. Of course, in the day-to-day progress of our lives, it is important to know exactly what rights are recognized. For the purposes of understanding the basis of our way of life, however, what is important is the idea that a set of individual rights belonging to every person does, in fact, exist.

There have been several changes over time in the meaning of the word *person,* to whom rights belong. Even now, the concept of individual rights does not extend to a huge part of our population—namely, to people under the age of 18. Only at the age of majority do people become fully *persons* before the law.

The second root idea is political democracy: All decisions governing a community are decided by the community in a politically democratic way. The first root idea, of individual rights, covers those actions in a people's lives that primarily affect themselves, and for which they are individually responsible. The second root idea, of political democracy, covers those actions that primarily affect groups of people, and for which they are responsible. The general principle is that the people most affected by an action should participate in deciding on it.

There is no single definition of the words *politically democratic decision making.* Essentially, they refer to a process by which issues are decided by vote and not by decree.

The third root idea is equal opportunity: Every person has an equal chance to obtain any goal. Equal opportunity does not, of course, mean an equal outcome for everybody. We have insisted on giving everyone the same starting line and then having people run where and how they wish; we have not insisted on making everyone run together in step. In Abraham Lincoln's memorable words, "[The Civil War] is essentially a People's contest. On the side of the Union, it is a struggle for maintaining in the world, that form and substance of government, whose leading object is, to elevate the condition of men—to lift artificial weights from all shoulders—to clear the paths of laudable pursuit for all—to afford all, an unfettered start, and a fair chance, in the race for life."

These three root ideas are inseparable from each other and from our country's fate. They are the American dream. To the extent that they are practiced, the American dream becomes the American reality.

One would think that our schools would be the most persistent and vigorous expounders of the American dream. After all, what is the ultimate goal of education, if not to prepare the nation's youth for a lifetime of responsible, mature citizenship? And who is charged with implementing this goal, if not the nation's schools? How tragic, then, how ominous for our future, that our educational system is the most un-American institution in this country today.

Students in our schools, from prenursery to postgraduate levels, have virtually no individual rights. They are almost entirely at the arbitrary mercy of teachers, staff, and administrators in everything they do at school. A student has no right of free speech, no right of dissent, no right of peaceful assembly, no right to confront his accuser, no right of privacy. The list can be extended to cover any and all of the traditional rights. During the entire formative period of their growth, youths are committed by law—and, after age 16, by economic and social pressure—to serve time in educational institutions that, like prisons, simply do not recognize the existence of individual rights. In the case of prisons, dealing with criminals and lawbreakers, one can certainly argue the merits of this situation one way or another, however uncertain the result. In the case of schools, one can only wonder at the "logic" that has led to this situation.

Does anyone really think that the way to prepare people for the responsible exercise and jealous guardianship of their rights is to raise them in an environment devoid of these rights? Would we for a moment do this in any other area? Would we expect a person to become literate in an environment devoid of the printed word? Would we expect someone to learn moral conduct among a gang of criminals?

If individual rights are barely known in schools, political democracy is even further removed from the realities of school life. In no area of our educational system does decision-making take place according to the tenets of political democracy. In fact, our educational system is the only major institution in the country that officially recognizes autocracy as its principle of government. Schools categorically deny that the people affected by decisions should be the ones making these decisions. Students are not the primary determiners of what they learn and how they should behave in school; they do not even have a voice in these matters.

The schools are almost a perfect model of political autocracy. There is a well-defined hierarchy, a clear chain of command. Each level has almost unlimited control over the next level below, the student being at the bottom of the heap. There is no regular means of appeal, only the hope of moving someone higher up by playing on their good will. Rules and regulations are promulgated without the necessity for debate or consent. One predictable result of this setup is that the system is permeated with resentment and hatred, and at every level enormous energies are spent breaking or subverting the rules. The architects of our educational system apparently forgot one of the great benefits of political democracy: Laws created through the consent of those to whom they apply— government by the consent of the governed—gain a respect and a level of observance that no other system of laws can approach, not even one backed up by massive terror. The law you have helped to make is the one you will least readily break.

The absence of equal opportunity in our schools is well known in some areas but hardly appreciated in other areas that are far more significant. It is, for example, well known that the way our present schools are set up often leaves students belonging to a particular ethnic group, or a particular economic class, or living in a particular geographic location, at a terrible disadvantage relative to other students from the outset.

However, there are other, hidden, more sinister areas where the idea of equal opportunity is flouted, to everyone's detriment. These reside in a guidance system that aims to find out at an ever-earlier age—on the basis of tests, interviews, and background investigations—what course of life is "most suitable" for each student and to "help" direct each student along the path thus determined. A poor math student, such as Albert Einstein was in school, is hardly given a chance to major in physics! Equal opportunity means that every student expressing a wish to pursue a given course should be given the same chance to try it. A person's life destiny should be his or hers to decide, and the only guidance program consistent with our ideals is one that gives everyone the same chance at everything.

Our country can no longer afford to maintain its un-American schools. Neither the people who attend these schools, nor those who run them, nor those who have so long supported them can tolerate any longer the contradictions between what the schools stand for and what the country stands for.

The arguments against granting full civil rights to children, and empowering them to govern their own lives, have no basis in experience. They are the same stale arguments that were advanced against the extension of rights to African-American slaves, and later, after the passage of the Fourteenth Amendment settled that issue, to women. They are arguments that stem from preconceived prejudices and patronizing attitudes.

There is ample evidence that children are quite capable of being full citizens in a free society. For several generations, schools have existed in which children are treated as adults, and accorded the same respect as adults. Summerhill School in England was the first to try this approach, in the 1920s. Since then, dozens of new schools have sprung up all over the world, many of them identifying themselves as "democratic schools," others based on the Sudbury Valley School model.[28] These environments have succeeded in producing effective adult members of society, possessing the full panoply of character traits that one expects citizens of a liberal democracy to possess.

6

Factors That Resist Change

You are being taught by people who have been able to accommodate themselves to a regime of thought laid down by their predecessors. It is a self-perpetuating system. Those of you who are more robust and individual than others will be encouraged to leave and find ways of educating yourself—educating your own judgments. Those that stay must remember, always, and all the time, that they are being moulded and patterned to fit into the narrow and particular needs of this particular society.

—Doris Lessing

Teachers, like employees of any system, try to ensure their job security. They do so in the educational system by requiring students to be taught the subjects they, the teachers, know. *Required* courses in different subjects are the product of teachers at all levels of schooling acting to preserve the need for their services. This is true even when what they teach is not required for students to perform well in an industrial society. Suppose a certain group of teachers know history. Their efforts to achieve employment security has led them, for example, to assert that it is very important for every student to know history, even though they don't need that knowledge to run a machine effectively. Because students are already in school, teaching them stuff such as history can be rationalized by asserting that it makes for good citizenship and more-rounded individuals. The same is true for biology, for foreign language, and so on. Curricula are built up in this way.

Faculty keep adding to the curricula they offer to provide employment to an increasing (and increasingly varied) group of teachers. To make this happen requires a huge educational bureaucracy that becomes entrenched, usually (but not exclusively) in the local government and in the private sector. Thousands of people work on designing courses, writing textbooks, administering exams, maintaining records, and so on. Today, more people are involved in this education-industrial complex than there are even in the military-industrial complex. The result is that schools teach material to children who never asked for it, don't need it, and don't even service machines any longer. The Industrial Revolution has been contracting continuously and has almost completely disappeared. It is being replaced by a new era that has entirely different people needs to be filled by the educational process.

The explosion in the number of employees working in the educational system is awesome, and worrisome. A spiral effect has all but whirled out of control. It began in colleges and universities, which have convinced the public that anyone who does not obtain a college degree is destined to be a "loser" in today's society. (It is hard to remember that a mere half century ago, a huge proportion of the population did not even finish high school, let alone go to college.) This has created both a demand for more colleges and a need for jobs fulfilling the conditions that a college education promised. Staffing all the colleges with professors, teaching assistants, deans, and administrators satisfies some of the employment needs. In Philadelphia, for example, the University of Pennsylvania is the largest employer. Because schools have traditionally been places of employment for people with some degree of formal education, they became the obvious source of new jobs.

It would appear at first blush that, given the finite number of children in schools, the number of job openings in schools would be limited. It turned out, however, that this was not at all the case: Schools held out the promise for an almost limitless number of new employees, by creating a wide variety of new openings, of which the following are but a sampling:

- More regular teachers, so that class size can be reduced, there being no lower limit to the desirable teacher/student ratio until the ideal of one-to-one has been reached. The dogma of "smaller classes mean better learning" has been disproved by repeated studies, but the movement for smaller classes has not in the least abated.[29]

- More subjects introduced into the curriculum as "absolutely essential" for the education of the young, thus creating a need for whole new categories of teachers. The multiplication of courses also leads directly to the need for an army of "specialists" whose function it is to fill in the inevitable gaps in the knowledge of classroom teachers, given the additional subject matter that must be covered. Technological developments have generated not only new courses and curricula, but even new departments in universities, too.

- Ever-increasing monitoring of the effectiveness of teaching, through the administration of tests in classrooms at every age level. This creates a burgeoning industry of testing and "research."

- Increased testing also leads, by its very nature, to "discovery" of an increasing number of students who fall below the desired level of achievement (despite the clearly expressed goal, mocked by Garrison Keillor, that every student be "above average"). This in turn spawns an enormous effort in "remedial" education, aimed at raising test scores—an effort that embraces not only special tutors and after-school classes, but also counselors, school psychologists, and specialized personnel whose function it is to develop and administer medications that affect the ability of students to perform in the precise manner that the schools require.

What is sad is the fact that this entire growing industry has been developed around a system of education that is basically obsolete, and one that no longer serves the needs of the children growing up to face the world of the twenty-first century. It is sobering to consider the unsettling effect that the not-so-gradual dismantling of this educational system will have on the large number of employees who will no longer be serving a useful function in society. We have already seen similar societal upheavals in the transition that has occurred in the world of industrial production.

The reluctance to change any system, including the educational system, in any fundamental way derives to a large extent from something done to us in school. All through school, we are shown that making a mistake is a bad thing, something for which we are downgraded. This reveals how little conventional schools are interested in learning, because we never learn by doing something right; we already know how to do it. Doing it right does confirm what we already know, and this has some value, but it contributes nothing to learning.

We can only learn experientially from our mistakes, by identifying and correcting them. But schools seldom give us an opportunity to do this; when a mistake is made and graded, it is indelible. So, we learn that mistakes are to be avoided at all costs.

This attitude is carried over to our jobs after schooling because most organizations also abhor mistakes and, like school, punish for making them.

But, there are two kinds of mistakes: errors of commission and errors of omission. Errors of commission consist of doing something that should not have been done. Errors of ommission consist of not doing something that should have been done. Of these, errors of omission are usually the most costly because it is harder to correct a missed opportunity than to correct something that has been done.

The accounting systems that all our institutions, public and private, employ record only errors of commission, the lesser in importance. Errors of omission are not recorded, and therefore, neither is their cost. Thus, those who want to avoid errors in an organization that takes mistakes to be a bad—if not punishable—thing find that to maximize their job security they should do as little as possible. To protect themselves further, they try to ensure that mistakes that are made are not attributed to them. This consists of passing the buck, absolution from accountability. This is the source of the conservatism that pervades in our society and its institutions today.

The two kinds of mistakes are closely linked, and the link is significant. A main reason people make mistakes of omission is that they are afraid of making a mistake of commission. The reason I don't do something I should (a mistake of omission) is that I am afraid that by doing it I will be doing something I shouldn't (a mistake of commission). Eliminating the fear of mistakes of commission goes a long way to solving the problem of mistakes of omission.

If we are to bring about institutional changes of a fundamental (transformative) nature, we must change the prevailing attitude toward mistakes. The attitude we should seek was beautifully captured in a statement (paraphrased here) that August Busch III, then CEO of Anheuser-Busch companies, made to his subordinates: If you didn't make a serious mistake last year, it probably indicates that you didn't try anything fundamentally new. You need not fear that making such a mistake will be held against you. But, making the same mistake twice will be.

PART 2

Factors That Contribute to Education

The principal goal of education... should be creating men and women who are capable of doing new things, not simply repeating what other generations have done; men and women who are creative, inventive and discoverers, who can be critical and verify, and not accept, everything they are offered.

—Jean Piaget

7

The Environment a Developed Society Provides for Individual Realization

Do I dare set forth here the most important,
the most useful rule of all education?
It is not to save time, but to squander it.

—Jean-Jacques Rousseau

Every human being is a unique member of our species, possessor of a sense of inner purpose; nevertheless, this soul of ours finds its expression in a real life that is conducted within the framework of a larger culture. The way each person finds meaning in life is intimately related to the environment within which that person resides. Stated differently, we can say that the surrounding culture serves to define the parameters of a meaningful life, the broad outline of the range of activities that it will accept, welcome, or tolerate within its midst. (In any given society, people who insist that their calling is one that lies beyond the furthest boundaries tolerated by that society are excluded from the society, either by being labeled insane—and thus shunted aside—or by being forcibly evicted, if not executed.)

The activities sought, needed, or tolerated by a given culture are defined not only by the traditional life stories of the members of the culture, but also, and quite critically, by the extent to which the culture interacts with other cultures located beyond its farthest geographic reaches. From earliest times, as the archeological evidence amply attests, there existed communication between various societies that were somehow physically connected to each other. With each successive advance in the efficiency of human transportation—from travel by foot, to the use of domesticated animals as load bearers, to the steady improvement of modes of water travel—more societies came to affect one another and influence each other's development; and with this process came a broadening of the range of each individual's potential dreams and aspirations for his or her life.

In addition, growing affluence allowed the emergence of a degree of leisure for many individuals that, in turn, gave them the freedom to spend their time in activities that transcended the bare struggle for physical survival. The transformation of hunter-gatherer societies to agricultural societies provided hitherto unimaginable opportunities for ways of life—careers, as we have come to call them—that could provide deep satisfaction to individuals and welcome additions to the community's cultural store. One need only compare the variety of life stories in a modern hunter-gatherer community with that of any ancient agricultural society to realize the explosion of options available to persons growing up in the latter compared to the former.

As far as we can tell from surviving records and archeological data, from the earliest historic times (defined as times from which written records have survived), some 10,000 years ago, a large number of different cultures were in some form of communication with each other, from the farthest reaches of Asia to North Africa and most of Europe. Land caravans and wide-ranging seafaring made such interlinkages possible. This development meant that leisure classes throughout this expansive region were able to dream of all sorts of exotic personal destinies.[30] Thus, an Alexander of Macedonia, growing up in a political environment of small city-states, could imagine his destiny to be that of the conqueror of the entire world and could take concrete steps to realize his destiny. A Marco Polo, some 1,500 years later, could dream of travel by land to the farthest reaches of the East and turn his dream into reality.

The age of modern science, and its offspring, the industrial age (which, together, have been labeled "modern times"), brought about a second radical change in the human condition of those societies that participated actively in the unfolding of these overlapping eras (often referred to as "developed societies")—and, gradually, in other communities throughout the world that came into contact with them. To fully comprehend this change, and the effect it had on people born into developed societies, it is necessary to examine the key elements of modern science and modern technology.

The goal of science is, and has always been, comprehension of the workings of the world that we experience. Aptly called "natural philosophy" until recently, science focuses on the perceptible environment and tries to make sense of it. Every known human culture has engaged in the taxing endeavor of understanding the functioning of the cosmos; science, understood broadly, is a universal human activity.

The ancient Greeks introduced a new feature into the practice of natural philosophy. Gradually, over a period of several centuries, thinkers from towns all over the widespread Greek-speaking domain of settlement created a novel method of thinking about nature—and, by extension, about human affairs. The participation of so many ancient Greek philosophers from so many far-flung city-states is testimony to the enriching effect personal interactions have on cultural development. The early philosophers and their disciples traveled from city to city and were eagerly engaged by their local counterparts. We have many beautiful examples of this process in Plato's dialogues and a great deal of surviving evidence concerning the slow process of developing rational thought.

The new Greek way of thinking was labeled "rational thought" and was informed by the notion that the only valid way of looking at the world was through the lens of "reason" or "logic." As applied to the physical universe, natural philosophy embodied the application of rational analysis to the world of perception. Greek science demanded rigorous use of both logic and careful observation in the formulation of scientific theory.

This marriage of analysis and meticulous observation (including active experimentation) eventually became widely accepted throughout the Western world, and later the Islamic world, and remained virtually intact for almost 2,000 years. It formed the inspiration for the vast store of useful knowledge accumulated in those cultures and was the basis for the huge advances in technology that occurred over the span of those two millennia.

Modern science introduced a radically new element into natural philosophy, superimposed on the two existing foundations: the element of fantasy, otherwise known by its more acceptable name, "imagination." The major contribution of the giants of early modern science—Copernicus, Kepler, Galileo, Newton, to name but a few—and the many others who laid the foundation for modern science was the idea that a key element of the process of gaining an understanding of the natural world was the ability to engage in flights of fancy about how things interacted and changed over time. Once the imagination was unleashed, concepts such as a heliocentric planetary system, forces that act at a distance, gravity, and the aether burst forth in a rich plethora of exciting and phantas-magoric potential explanatory schemes for natural phenomena. The genie of imagination in scientific endeavor multiplied its efforts as time went on, leading to the current scientific environment in which the relationship between fundamental concepts and direct, unmediated perception has all but been abandoned.[31]

The core idea of the industrial age was equally simple and revolutionary—and, in fact, equally fantastic. It was the socioeconomic notion that it was possible to provide the entire population with the ability to rise above a grueling struggle for survival and to enjoy instead the benefits of material abundance and the good health and leisure that flow therefrom. In place of the widespread acceptance of grinding poverty as the lot of most people in this life ("you shall eat bread by the sweat of your brow"), and the accompanying hope of a better fate in the afterlife, the industrial age held forth the possibility for a good life here on Earth—the possibility that all people could dream about realizing their inner destinies in this world. As might be expected, advances in technology in nearly every aspect of human existence were accompanied by an outpouring of writings on social and economic theory, which has only increased in volume in the intervening years.[32]

Unfortunately, theory and practice lagged far behind the fantasy of the promise. Machines were too stupid, and the ironic reality of the industrial age was that the struggle for survival of the great masses in the agricultural era was simply replaced by a similar struggle for the masses of industrial workers. In addition, as we have discussed, the needs of the industrial age led to the imposition of a system of schooling that provided the necessary human adjunct to the industrial machine.[33]

It was left to the post-industrial era, which dawned in the latter half of the twentieth century, to make it possible for the promise of modern times to be a reality for all people. This realization is only now, in the early years of the twenty-first century, beginning to take hold of the imagination and aspiration of much of humanity, with drastic and chaotic sociopolitical consequences. It has, however, permeated the cultures of industrially developed countries.

Let us look, then, at what our era offers virtually all its inhabitants—features that were hitherto reserved for the few. As we list them, we should note their interconnectedness; they are not an independent group of features that by some coincidence appeared together on the stage of history. They form an interrelated complex that defines our times.

The ability to access up-to-date knowledge directly on a global scale. This stems not only from the very recent invention of the Internet, and the many improvements in its scope and usability that are issuing forth in a steady stream, but also from other significant factors:

- Huge advances in publishing that make the distribution of written material more rapid and more easily achievable than ever

- Rapid advances in audio and video communication, either person to person or group to group, potentially on a worldwide basis

- The growing availability of rapid forms of relatively inexpensive transportation that make face-to-face interactions feasible as never before

- And, the explosive increase in the capacity for information storage and retrieval, in fixed and portable forms

One need only compare the situation to that which prevailed half a century ago, when virtually all the factors listed here did not exist or existed at best in primitive form.

The ability to access the finest archetypes of practice in any field. Consider this: Until the 1920s, it was impossible for budding musicians to hear performances by the world's best musicians; even if they lived in a great metropolis, only a few exemplars could be heard at best and then only on rare occasions. Hence the multiplicity of third-rate music teachers and students all over the world and the difficulty of rising to new heights of excellence. Compare the situation today, when the best and the worst are available at a click; and compare the number of excellent performances, individual and group, that occur in towns and cities all over the developed world. Think of any field: You can see the best politicians in action, read the finest speeches delivered anywhere, observe stellar courtroom performances and peruse the legal briefs filed by the best lawyers, study three-dimensional designs of the most admired architects, and so on. Self-evaluation, which depends critically on accessibility to models and archetypes, takes a leap forward; people now have the potential to measure themselves against the best.

The ability to interact with others, anywhere, who share common interests. Ideas never develop in a vacuum; everyone needs a foil against whom to test one's ideas, and with whom to share the latest news, to laugh at the latest follies, to speculate about the future, to delve deeply into the past. "No man is an island unto himself"—and today, in developed societies (and even elsewhere), every man has at his disposal bridges from his place of individuality to the places of any other individual who wants to engage in an exchange with him. Situations that were once limited to salons, to seminars, to private soirees, to social gatherings, are now open electronically to all who wish to take advantage of them. Who can count the number of chat rooms and instant messages in place at any given time?

The ability to disseminate widely new ideas, inventions, and artistic creations. So you have a brainstorm, something exciting to show, a new composition to play. No problem. Put it on your web page (billions exist, billions more will be created every year), build in a tie-in to a search engine, and you are on your way. Make CDs or DVDs, publish short-run books, and talk them up in electronic forums. Never before has it been so easy to spread innovation. What might have taken years or decades to come to light a century ago (or never come to light at all) today shines forth in an instant. It wasn't that long ago that new scientific discoveries had to await publication in a peer-review journal. And it wasn't *that* long ago (just the early nineteenth century) that Sadi Carnot's second law of thermodynamics languished for two decades before anyone else heard about it,[34] and his anticipation of the law of conservation of energy was buried in unpublished notebooks that did not come to light for more than a hundred years!

The ability to receive immediate feedback for any contributions to the culture. Not only can you get the word out, but you can get the word back, too! Customer reviews, reader reviews, viewer reviews, and so on are common these days on commercial Internet sites; feedback, and feedback to the feedback, is the stuff of the exponentially increasing number of blogs; and e-mail provides rapid and personal response where public forums are not wanted. All this is new. No longer does one wait anxiously for the major media outlets for a make-or-break review—reviews (whether good or bad) that were rarely granted to the great majority of ideas and creations. This enables a person caught up in the creations of his spirit to keep the momentum going, with the knowledge that the rough edges will be smoothed out by direct and immediate criticisms.

The ability to locate and approach sources of funding for enterprises that require financial backing. Money, so often necessary to proceed with one's life enterprise and so difficult to find! Once upon a time, not that long ago, financing a dream faced almost insurmountable barriers, because the sources of funds were all channeled through a small number of governmental agencies, private foundations, corporate sponsors, venture capitalists, or investment banks. Politics, the arts, science, and business were more often than not held hostage to a small band of people who held the purse strings. The same sources of funding still exist, still try to exert control over the culture, but the new avenues of direct communication have allowed the emergence of altogether new financial supporters. Slowly, inevitably, the stranglehold held by banks, by large corporations, by major political donors, and by well-endowed foundations is being loosened. Small-time supporters, banding together, are gathering funds that enable innovators in all domains to move forward unhampered by traditional constraints. With every passing year, the liberating effect of this phenomenon is being felt in society.

The ability to create situations—businesses, in the general meaning of the term—in or out of the mainstream that support one's dreams, and that have the potential to reap financial rewards. In most developed societies, it is easier to start a business enterprise—proprietary, partnership, corporation—than ever before. The realization that private enterprise provides an opportunity for innovation to march forward without concern for undue regulation has long been at the heart of the American economic system and has been central to most developed countries. Those that have not allowed private enterprise to flourish have learned through bitter experience the cost to their ability to remain part of the modern world. This has little to do with political theory or form of government; private enterprise is simply a society's way of validating individuals' burning desire to set their own goals and strive to meet them.

The ability to find existing places of employment that will support one's calling. The fact that it is easier than ever to strike out on one's own, especially for people with initiative and motivation, has caused a major change to take place in traditional places of employment. Existing employers realize today that to remain viable, they have to be able to attract and keep among their work force a large contingent of people who want to be there and who feel that they can each, individually, lead meaningful lives within the framework offered by the employers. People who feel a burning desire to realize themselves have a better chance than ever to find a place of employment that is seeking precisely such people.

The ability to develop one's interests to any level of attainment one desires, at a pace that is suitable to one's character. For all the reasons already stated, there is no upper limit to the degree of excellence people can reach if they so desire. More important, because the path to such excellence can be determined and controlled by the individual, given the tools available today, there is no predetermined time frame for this progress from stage to stage. Because people can choose their calling, and find the level to which they aspire, free of external constraints, they can also choose the length of time they devote to traversing their paths. Nobody is holding them on a leash or pushing them along with a prod. The factor of time has become less relevant than ever before. We have always adopted this approach to people of recognized genius; we know that there is no hurrying them along. In an era that now allows everyone's personal genius to develop, there is no need to keep an eye on the calendar clock for anyone. This trend has been strengthened by the steady lengthening of human life spans in developed societies.

The ability to move from one activity to another during their lives. In our "time of rapid change"—a phrase that has become a cliché only in recent decades—few things are static. Today, we have finally come to *expect* change and have no sense of surprise when major new developments occur. Industries come and go, corporations rise and fall, scientific breakthroughs become obsolete overnight, and major technological advances follow each other at breakneck speed. Heraclitus finally emerges as the philosopher who most clearly understood the world: "All is change." Not only is the river you stepped in today different from the one you stepped in yesterday: The DVD player of today, the automobile of today, the theory of matter of today, the medical paradigm of today, the miracle medicine of today—all are different from the ones of yesterday, and at least as different from the ones of tomorrow. With a rapidly changing environment, people will also undergo changes in the way they realize themselves in life. My destiny manifests itself in one set of actions now, but in the world of a decade from now, my same inner calling may manifest itself in a different context. The culture of the modern world is one that invites, and welcomes, an ever-changing and evolving life story for each individual. People with a single lifelong career will be the exception rather than the rule that they were up until now. A person may still be called the same thing all her life—for example, professor, or chief executive officer, or medical doctor—but the person will rarely be actualizing her calling in the same manner over the span of a lifetime.

Taken together, these features completely obviate any perceived need to force the great mass of individuals into a narrow range of activities that once defined the entire spectrum of activities available to them in society.

The range of activities is now unlimited, both in content and in place. Predictability is gone. The unbounded limits of the human imagination, recognized 500 years ago as a prerequisite to the development of human knowledge, are now open to all comers.

The information age offers historically new opportunities to every person. As we shall see, it is now possible for education to revert to its initial meaning of finding a meaningful life for each individual within the context of the greater culture. In addition, now, for the first time in history, the greater culture is global and offers more opportunity for variety, for creativity, and for diversity than ever before.

The environment of a developed society may also present obstructions to individual realization, as when it treats different groups within the society differentially. For example, the opportunities for individual realization are often quite different for people in poor urban or rural settings from those for people in wealthier settings. Education should be as concerned with overcoming the obstructions as taking advantage of the opportunities. Therefore, a principal function of education should be to enable those who are the most obstructed to overcome the obstructions, to reveal how society should be changed to remove such obstructions.

The rise of the dependence on rational thought was harmful in many situations. Rationality was believed to be an absolute property of thought, not relative. Thus, for example, for many years in the latter half of twentieth century, the Ford Foundation tried to reduce the birthrate in India. It correctly perceived that as long as the birthrate exceeded the rate of growth of the national economy, poverty would increase. Nevertheless, its efforts at controlling the birthrate completely failed. The foundation's executives attributed this to the irrationality of the Indians. "Couldn't they understand that failure to reduce the birthrate was the cause of increasing poverty?"

It did not occur to them that the birthrate was rational from the Indian family's point of view. There was no form of social security in India, but the expectation of most males was they would experience a long period (about 20 years) of unemployment after their late 30s because of increasing life spans and more males available than jobs. They would not survive without children to support them. It turned out that the size of most Indian families was exactly that required to provide enough employable males to support an unemployed father and mother. The Indians were completely rational given their expectations and their environment, not Ford's.

The industrial age not only "held forth the possibility for a good life here on Earth," but it also increased life expectancy dramatically. It increased from about 27 years in the Middle Ages, to the current upper 70s. When life expectancy was only 27 years, and these years were usually spent under miserable conditions, people's focus was naturally on the "afterlife." An eventual, infinitely extended afterlife in paradise received more attention than the miserable life here and now. The extension of life expectancy changed this focus to the here and now, and this contributed to the development of science.

Many advantages that our era presents bear within them the seeds of a related disadvantage; avoiding the latter then becomes a problem to be solved. For example, it is true that we have better access to information and knowledge today than at any previous time in history. Relevant information is more readily available than it ever was. However, those who have to make decisions may at times be handicapped by an overabundance of irrelevant information that makes it difficult to sort out the relevant information.

Furthermore, the alleged knowledge produced by experts is frequently used to manipulate people for the advantage of the manipulators.[35] In addition, the ability to access the finest archetypes of practice in any field can encourage the production of fads and panaceas that are widely adopted to no avail.

The ability to interact with others who share common interests is certainly an advantage that has been increased in our era. However, it has also increased the ability to interact with those of opposing interests and values. Has this increased or decreased conflict? Increased communication is of value only if those involved have compatible objectives. Often, the more and better information that enemies at war have about each other, the more harm they can inflict on each other. In such a case, better communication means worse results.

It is certainly true that modern technology makes it possible to obtain reviews of one's ideas more rapidly and in greater number. However, this is not always a good thing. The quality of reviews transmitted through current technology leaves much to be desired. The quality of a review depends, of course, on the quality of its source. In many cases, this essential information is not available to the recipient of reviews.

Although sources of funding are more numerous, so are those competing for their funds. With more funding available, it is easier to start new businesses and other types of organizations. Nevertheless, most businesses do not survive their first year, and the average life of those that do is less than 15 years. It is not always the case that the ability to sustain an enterprise has increased in the current environment.

The increasing ability to change jobs is confronted with obstructions to doing so. For instance, such a change may involve a loss of health benefits or pension funds. Employees have found ways to tie down "good" employees (for example, stock options). The educational system does not stimulate development of the courage that makes criticism of employers common and the willingness to start over in a new work environment. In general, the educational system produces security seekers, not change promoters.

The ability to take advantage of the job flexibility currently available depends critically on the ability of the job-jumper to learn quickly what is required to succeed in the new work environment. What they know is not nearly as important as how quickly they can learn and their willingness to do so.

8

The Special Demands the Environment of a Liberal Democracy Places on Individual Realization

*If the education and studies of children were suited to
their inclinations and capacities,
many would be made useful members of society
that otherwise would make no figure in it.*

—Samuel Richardson

Viewing education as the individual's lifelong path toward realizing his or her destiny appears, at first sight, to be a selfish view of humanity, one that emphasizes personal gratification even at the expense of others. Such a conclusion would be widely off the mark, for a simple reason: Just as human beings are, each and every one, born with an innate desire to lead a meaningful life, so too are they born with an innate desire to connect with other people. Humans are, by nature, social animals, and creating a satisfactory social setting for one's life is as important as creating a purposeful existence. Education thus turns out to have another aspect to it—namely, an aspect of learning to develop relationships between the individual and the society in which that individual resides. Thus, although the socioeconomic structure of a developed society in the twenty-first century allows virtually unlimited opportunities for a wide variety of individual life stories, the social realities of the surrounding culture may place limitations, or impose requirements, on the activities of its members.[36]

A tension always exists between the individual and the community within which that individual lives. People are born with a strong desire · to find their unique place in the world, but at the same time, they are born with a strong social instinct that leads them to seek out other people and form friendships and associations.

The inherent ability of humans to create complex languages—a skill that attains a level far beyond that of any other species—is itself the ultimate expression of the people's need for mutual interaction. A key purpose of language is to exchange thoughts among people. From the earliest age, children seek to express themselves through language, and thus to integrate themselves into the social group around them. But, even as language is a tool from which children, and adults, benefit as individuals by tapping into the minds of other people, so too language is the means by which the world outside the individual expresses its needs and constraints to the individual. Language is a two-edged sword: an invaluable aid to each person in his or her lifelong development, but also an instrument of control exerted by society over each of its members.[37]

For most of history, agricultural societies adopted hierarchical social structures based on coercion by a ruling class. (This is true even of ancient democracies, such as that of Athens, in which the ruling class was simply larger than usual, but nevertheless a small fraction of the population of the community as a whole; the rest consisted of women, slaves, and children.) In such an environment, the freedom of action allotted to each person depends on his or her place in the power structure or on the individual's personal relationship to members of the power structure. Limitations on the freedom to pursue personal life goals are more the norm than the exception for all but an elite. The vast majority of people abandon the dreams and aspirations of their youth; for them, education in the true sense of the term was an unreal fantasy, replaced by the forced learning of specific skills required for survival. Whether bound to the land as serfs, or drafted as soldiers, or forced into servitude, their individuality was submerged by the demands of those who dominated the community.

A new concept of social organization emerged slowly over the past 500 years or so, inspired by the governmental model invented and developed in England. This has been endowed with the generic name "liberal democracy," whose precise meaning has been, and continues to be, evolving.

As we have seen, three philosophical concepts lie at the heart of the idea of liberal democracy. One is the notion that all members of a society have the same inherent worth as human beings—embodied in the slogan "all men are created equal." This notion demands equal respect for the lives and aspirations of all members of the society who live within the broad limits of permissible action defined by the society. It is the ultimate expression of nondiscrimination on any basis whatsoever.

The second is the notion that the only legitimate way for a society to define its rules, its limits of permissible action, is through mechanisms that allow equal participation of all people in the decision-making process that defines those rules—"government through the consent of the governed"; "government of the people, by the people, for the people."

The third principle is that there exist certain domains of personal action that are off-limits to societal control and fundamentally protected from interference by societal rules—"inalienable rights."

Thus, a liberal democracy dances around the tension between individual and society in a subtle, intricate choreography, weaving in and out of the ever-changing bounds of equality, community self-government, and individual rights. The complexity of the interaction between these three basic principles forms the framework of the evolution of liberal democracies, and the setting in which humanity continues to progress over time.[38]

A noteworthy aspect of liberal democracy is that it can be viewed as the only way individual empowerment can be reconciled with social restrictions, because it is unique in basing those restrictions on a foundation of empowerment.

From a historical perspective, it is remarkable that the conceptual underpinnings for liberal democracy as a viable social system were first, if haltingly, formulated in England, a typically hierarchical society with little to distinguish it from others contemporary to it; and later elaborated, in the eighteenth century, in France, perhaps one of the more extreme examples of a society whose structure was diametrically opposite to that of a liberal democracy. However, liberal democracy did not emerge in its stable form until the strange and unique North American experiment expressed itself in the American Revolution and in the political creations of the Founding Fathers of the United States. Apparently, only a culture that was oceans apart from all its roots, geographically and socially, could imagine for itself the task of creating a wholly new sociopolitical environment, picking and choosing from among the components at hand to create an original system that combined them into a consistent, integrated whole.

Education in a liberal democracy thus involves people finding a way to realize their unique destinies in the social context defined by the three concepts previously outlined. People must learn for themselves how to achieve their personal goals in a setting that protects their sacred rights and in a manner that accords full respect for their fellow beings and is consistent with rules that they had a part in establishing.

How can this be done? The most direct way is through immersion and the ongoing life experience that occurs through immersion. How to integrate a person's individual aspirations with those of the community within which that person lives is learned most easily by growing up immersed in the sociopolitical environment of a liberal democracy.

We have many examples of how hard it is to become educated in both senses (individual and social) when immersion is not available. Thus, the rather sudden appearance on the world scene of global communication and information transfer has catapulted many societies from medieval conditions to twenty-first-century conditions with traumatic speed.[39] The clash between their accustomed notions of the lives they may aspire to and the dazzling variety of new options now apparently open to them inevitably leads to immense personal and social upheavals and a pervasive sense of insecurity and rootlessness. Their own cultures seem under attack, and there is necessarily a profound internal conflict each member of those societies undergoes. That conflict is between hunkering down to defend the traditional cultures at all costs and abandoning their traditional cultures in favor of the new hitherto unknown opportunities beckoning to them from outside.

By the same token, societies catapulted from a long history of hierarchical sociopolitical organization into a world that admires liberal democracy inevitably face tremendous internal stresses that stem from their lack of experience with the philosophical principles of this new social order.

Individual education in societies that are wrenched forcibly, by the historical forces of cultural globalization, from their past into the present becomes an enormously challenging process for every person, child, or adult in those societies. It is almost impossible for those of us who have grown up in the United States, or in similar Western cultures, to imagine ways by which education can be nurtured in such alien settings.

By contrast, the relative ease of becoming educated by immersion is a blessing we in this country enjoy, through no effort of our own. We are surrounded daily by reminders of the broad range of individual opportunities available to us, and we have no need to exert ourselves unduly to discover them. Similarly, we live our lives in a liberal democracy proudly defined as "the cradle of liberty" and take for granted the blessings and the obligations our sociopolitical environment endows upon us.

In thinking, therefore, about education in our country, we must take into account the social aspects of education and the realities of immersion. It is not realistic or productive to ignore the value of immersion in a liberal democratic environment when we contemplate the ongoing viability of our social order. And it is downright counterproductive to think that placing individuals in a rigidly autocratic environment has value in enhancing the quality of their lives, or of the society as a whole, in a liberal democracy.

Language is not limited to the transmission of thoughts. It also transmits feelings, attitudes, observations, and so on. There is no mental content that cannot be transmitted by language.

There are many different versions of any language, differences in pronunciation, grammar, and vocabulary. These were and continue to be largely regional in nature. However, radio and television have had a major effect on standardizing speech across our nation. Regional accents have diminished over time. Nevertheless, some minorities tend to retain their own version of the language. This can be a major handicap for those who seek to advance in our society. The same is true for those immigrants and their progeny who retain their native language as their primary language.

If education is to provide immigrants, minorities, and their progeny equal opportunities for advancement in our society, it must enable them to speak and write in the prevailing version of our language. It should not discourage their possession and use of a second language. But, there should be recognition that citizenship in a country is significantly enhanced when there is a common language, even if it is not the first language of everyone.

The importance of knowing the meaning of commonly used words cannot be overemphasized. For example, one's definition of *democracy* is likely to have a major influence on one's politics. Here is mine, similar to the one previously given, but using different words to say the same thing—which may help enhance the understanding of the meaning we attribute to the word. I also use three conditions to define it:

1. Every person within a social group who may be affected by a decision made by that group can participate in making that decision, either directly or indirectly through representatives. If a person cannot for whatever reason participate in the selection of representatives to make such decisions, the representatives must be selected for them in a way approved of by the group.

   There are special cases (for example, the mentally ill, very young children, those yet to be born, and those in prison). A democratic society must ensure representation of their *legitimate* interests, too. A legitimate interest is one the satisfaction of which does not deprive any others of the ability to satisfy any of their legitimate interests. When the interests of those affected (for instance, the unborn) are not known, decisions that may affect them should allow them to keep their options open as much as possible.

2. Anyone in a position of authority over others is subject to their collective authority. In a democracy, the electorate is the ultimate source of authority. This means that in a democratic society authority is circular, not linear (top down).

   Many organizations in a democratic society—corporations, schools, hospitals, prisons, government agencies, and so on— are managed autocratically, not democratically.[40] Citizens of a democracy should be aware of and understand this apparent inconsistency. The fact that most schools are managed autocratically deprives students of learning about democracy from experiencing it. Therefore, they are not prepared to participate in a democratic society or organization.

   Some argue that democracy should be reserved for the educated. This argument is spurious. How can people be educated for democracy other than by experiencing it? The educational process should provide that experience.

Our nation professes to accept the statement that "all men are created equal." However, it is important to realize that those who penned this statement did not mean by it what we do today. Women and African Americans were excluded originally, and those who didn't own land were not given a voice. Our democracy has become more inclusive, but it would be a terrible mistake to believe that opportunities are currently equally distributed. We still have a way to go.

Unfortunately "all men are created equal" does not mean that literally, because it is obviously false. We are not all born with the same physical and mental capabilities. What the phrase does mean is that regardless of birth differences, all people should have equal opportunities. How they take advantage of these opportunities reflects their differences.

Put another way, the social and economic properties of progeny ideally should not be correlated with those of their parents. Poverty, segregation, and ignorance, for example, should not be inherited characteristics.

3. In a democracy, anyone can do whatever he or she wants to do provided that it does not affect anyone else adversely. If it does, agreement by those affected is required. Our society is still a long way from meeting this condition. Religious fervor often stimulates legislation that seeks to control what people do in privacy but that affects no one else.

Immersion is indeed the best way to promote commitment to providing equal opportunities. During World War II, I was sent to Officers' Candidate School in Australia. When I arrived, I was assigned to a tent that housed six, but only one other person had been assigned by the time I moved in. The next two candidates who arrived were African Americans. This made no difference to the two of us already in the tent. We greeted them as equals. However, the next two were southern whites who looked around the tent from the entrance, saw the African Americans, withdrew, and went to the captain responsible for tent assignments; they asked to be reassigned. The captain wanted to know why. They told him. He replied that they had the following choice: either accept the assignment or resign from the school. They accepted the tent assignment. Relationships in the tent were initially frigid but thawed slowly over time. In about two months, they were spending their free time together, even double-dating. They went through a complete transformation. Immersion had done it.

Until I moved into the center of Philadelphia, I had little contact with known homosexuals. Our house in town was one of three built around a small court and gated off from the street. Our next-door neighbors were two gay men, both high school teachers. They were the most friendly and supportive neighbors we had ever had. They became close friends. Their sexual orientation became irrelevant to us.

So again, immersion had changed attitudes. Schools have an opportunity to promote not only tolerance but also complete acceptance of those who "differ" from us.

9

What Individuals Contribute to Their Own Education

Man is endogenous, and education is his unfolding. The aid we have from others is mechanical, compared with the discoveries of nature in us. What is thus learned is delightful in the doing, and the effect remains.

—Ralph Waldo Emerson

Education is the lifelong process of pursuing the activities that give meaning to our lives. Given that education in a country such as ours takes place in the social context of a liberal democracy, the question arises: What tools do human beings possess by nature to enable them to engage in this process?

In the opening words of his groundbreaking treatise *Metaphysics* (which more accurately translates as *Foundations of Natural Philosophy*), Aristotle provided the starting point for the answer to this question. He stated, simply, "Human beings are curious by nature." He identified curiosity as the cornerstone of his own search for the meaning of the universe, the essential feature that characterized his own life, and a defining feature of all people: curiosity understood as an active force, always in play, driving individuals to action in their daily lives, from the moment they are born until the moment they die.

Anyone who has observed infants cannot help noticing the intensity of their curiosity. They are consumed by a passion to observe the world around them, to make sense out of it, to figure out how to operate within it, and to learn how to control as much of it as possible to their own benefit. This trait never departs from the human spirit. The images of children "getting into everything," of youngsters never ceasing their questions, of adolescents pushing limits and experimenting with risky behavior, of grown-ups tinkering and inventing and always seeking new experiences—these images are the archetypical ones for all of humanity. They illustrate a simple truth: There is no need to "stimulate" curiosity in people. If anything, one of society's most difficult tasks is to define the limits that circumscribe the extent to which members of a community can engage their curiosity. Keeping the genie of curiosity from getting totally out of the bottle all of the time is a major preoccupation of institutions set up to manage the viable functioning of societies.

Curiosity keeps the individual in motion, always seeking change and innovation. It does not, however, give direction to motion, nor does it contain within it the skills to maintain motion. The key factor operating to produce tendencies in our behavior is our character, an entity that has been recognized from time immemorial and that, despite the focused study of countless great thinkers, has remained one of the great mysteries of the world.

We take it for granted that every individual has a unique character. It is character that accounts for our passions, for our determination to overcome challenges, for our interactions with others, and for many of our choices minute to minute and throughout our lifetime. Every parent recognizes almost from the moment of birth the special uniqueness of each newborn child's personality. It shows in the way they move, nurse, look, listen, cry, sleep, and in just about every manifestation of their being. How often do we hear it said of the young, "I just don't know where that child came from! S/he just isn't like any of us"? Adults who have grown up in the same home environment, attended the same schools, lived together in the same town, shared friends, invariably turn out to have unique and fundamentally different personalities.

The elements of character (to the extent that they can be classified separately, not taking into account their organic interrelationship) provide specific tools for a person's education. Here are some examples, with emphasis placed on children, although equally applicable to adults:

Passion provides the fire, the energy, to identify and pursue goals actively. No child is devoid of burning desires for something—playing a game over and over, collecting shells, climbing everything in sight, being read to or reading, watching cartoons, exploring woods, daydreaming. The variety is infinite; the common denominator is determination to follow the passion, with little consideration for time or effort.

Determination provides the stamina to stay the course, regardless of cost or obstacles. An infant learning to crawl is the archetype of this character trait. If you think about the physical process of crawling—the number of muscles, nerve fibers, joints, and visual and tactile inputs that have to be integrated properly to attain propulsion through crawling—it is almost impossible to figure out how this task can ever be achieved, at an age when the functions of all these factors are entirely new to the child. (For comparative purposes, think of how hard it is for us, as adults, to learn to ski, or even how to operate a backhoe.) For days, weeks, often months, nearly every child struggles to learn how to crawl. The goal is propulsion, which gives them the ability to reach out to their environment, explore it, and gain access to the objects of their desire. Despite repeated poor performance, often marked by spectacular failure (backward motion rather than the wished-for forward motion, rollover, collapse, and so forth), despite endless hours of wearying effort, despite the goal often seeming hopelessly out of reach, every child exhibits the trait of determination to succeed. Early childhood is filled with similar examples: the child learning to walk, to speak, to manipulate food, to control elimination, to sustain successful social interactions with adults and peers.

Confidence provides an internal steadying hand, reassuring people that their efforts to attain their individual goals are worth taking and have a good chance for success. Confidence also provides the stimulus for starting over when the desired ends have not been reached and new passions have to be discovered and pursued. Without confidence, a person might deem the struggle of day-to-day existence futile, not worthwhile. Confidence can be said to be the spark of life.

It may seem odd to claim that every child—every person—exhibits the character trait of confidence. One of the ubiquitous complaints you hear is that bad parenting, inadequate schools, political uncertainty, and poor living conditions undermine and destroy people's confidence, leading to widespread despair. This complaint misses the point. It addresses a narrow view of this trait as a feeling that one can succeed in living a lifestyle generally approved by the culture's self-appointed opinion makers. Thus, a child who feels that "I have what it takes to be a successful scientist" is considered to display confidence, as opposed to one who feels that "Nothing I do works out."

However, this is a narrow view of the trait. A broader, deeper view realizes that, as exhibited almost universally, confidence represents the feeling that "I have the ability to carry on somehow, no matter how devastating my life experience." It enables slaves to make it through another day, concentration camp inmates to face their tormentors,[41] laid-off workers to think about what they'll do next; it enables all those in despair to somehow go on with life, clinging to the belief that a more tolerable life may be attainable, that their existence might not be in vain after all.

Curiosity and character provide key innate tools for every person's education. There are many others. One is the *ability to analyze and solve problems*. What this means can most easily be understood by considering again the example of the infant learning to crawl. At first, his movements are random, a chaotic collection of arms and legs and hither and yon and nowhere. After a while, the collection begins to become more coordinated, and progression takes place. At some point, the child might be propelled in an unusual direction, opposite to the one he has become accustomed to. Initially, confusion reigns. More attempts are made. Some are satisfactory—the direction the child had come to expect—and some are not. Then, it dawns on the child that *there is a problem*. The *concept of a problem* emerges, the realization that "I wanted to do one thing, but another thing happened, and *this is a problem!*" Upon this realization, a question follows: What exactly is the nature of the problem, and how do I solve it?

Of course, we are talking here about preverbal children, and they are obviously not articulating what I have just outlined. But, they are acting in a manner that indicates that these thought processes are in fact taking place, in one form or another. Furthermore, the fact that children ultimately figure out how to crawl effectively demonstrates that they have within them the ability to solve problems. And, this ability turns out to be characteristic of all people at every age.[42]

Plainly put, it is no more necessary to teach people "problem solving" than it is to teach people breathing. Every human being develops his own approaches to solving problems, and does so naturally. This does not mean that we don't at times seek assistance from others whom we think can help us. But seeking assistance is, in itself, part of the skill of problem solving and, as you will see shortly, is something at which humans are uniquely talented.

Another innate tool worth noting is the *ability to contemplate*. "I think, therefore I am"; for Descartes, this tool is the essence of human existence. Although many of our actions come about as the result of habitual behavior, for the most part our lives consist of encountering situations that we have to think about, mull over, and integrate into our ever-developing understanding of the world.

Contemplation invokes a full panoply of emotional, aesthetic, and intellectual components. These come into play literally every moment of our lives. It not only appears in the obvious times. It appears when we see a beautiful sunset, when we read a book, when we daydream or "zone out," when we wonder about the meaning of life, when we ponder the origin of the universe, when we see a physically attractive person, and when we meet a new person or engage an old acquaintance. It is with us all our waking hours and even appears in our dreams.

Through contemplation, we form, test, add to, tweak, revise, and sometimes reject and restructure our individual *Weltanschauung* (worldview). It is the activity that enables us to exist as integrated personalities, filtering out the superfluous to hone in on those things we want to focus on and endow with relevance, from among the countless number of inputs that assault our senses at every moment. Its working can be seen in the youngest infants, whose eyes slowly learn to choose patterns that are meaningful to them, whose hands move incessantly to develop mental images of structure in the physical world, whose ears strain to create a distinction between cacophony and harmony. Every person, at every age, is at all times engaged in active thinking about their lives and their world.[43]

Perhaps the most powerful tool people possess by nature is the *ability to communicate*. (Saying that this is innate to all humans does not deny its presence in other animal species.) This ability is highly developed in our species and embraces many forms of interaction. They range from a wide variety of direct visual and emotional communication through body language, intonation, and physical contact, to the much more complex and rich form embodied by language.

The origin of language lies in the mind's ability to represent mental images—thoughts—by symbols. The nature of the link between these symbols and the thoughts behind them is mysterious, and a subject widely studied in a number of different disciplines.[44] Even more difficult to understand is the manner in which different people are able to attach meaning to each other's linguistic symbols—we shall refer to them simply as words, to encompass written, spoken, and sign languages—on a person-to-person basis, and within the wider boundaries of a community, social circle, nation, linguistic grouping, or multicultural setting. Whatever the mechanism by which language becomes a shared experience, the fact remains that the key benefit language provides to the process of an individual's lifelong education is the *ability to link into the thinking and learning of other people, and thereby to enrich vastly one's own ability to think and learn*. Language, in a very real sense, vastly enlarges the capability of my own mind to create meaning in my life, by potentially adding to my own resources the mental resources of the entire human race.

This fact has been true since the dawn of man as a species. As new forms of communicating linguistic symbols developed, the enhancing potential of language revealed itself in the development of increasingly superior systems of thought, of social organizations, of economic productivity, and of culturally enriched lifestyles. The invention of writing, of alphabets, of movable print, of mass production of paper and rapid methods of printing, of land-line electric information transfer, of wireless electronic communication, of audio-visual communication, of portable information storage on material media—each of these steps brought with them giant leaps in people's ability to educate themselves through the innate communication skills they, each and every one of them, possessed.

As discussed earlier, recent developments in cyberspace have made the potential inherent in interpersonal communication into a reality. Whereas, from the first emergence of the species, people had the inherent ability to communicate with any other member of our species, this ability has been transformed into the practical ability—not yet realized—to interact with virtually any other person in the world. The ultimate learning tool we possess—to communicate with others and thereby deeply enrich our educational opportunities—is now approaching its maximal potential of embracing within its scope the entire human race.

I agree that "human beings are curious by nature," but curiosity can be suppressed by external factors. It was seriously suppressed during the Middle Ages for a number of reasons, primarily because life expectancy was only about 27 years. A large percentage of the children born did not survive childhood, let alone infancy. Most of those who did survive lived in poverty and never traveled outside the small community in which they were born. Plague and pestilence were common. Under these conditions, many naturally asked, "What is the purpose of life?" The Catholic Church, the only institution of significant influence across Europe at that time, provided the answer: to prepare for the afterlife that could take place in Paradise and be infinitely extended. To get there, this life had to be lived according to the precepts of the Catholic Church. This discouraged concern with this life and focused attention on the one alleged to follow.

It took the Crusades and the beginnings of international trade and exploration to open society to external influences and encourage the revitalization of curiosity. Nevertheless, the suppression of curiosity continues even today in a very subtle way.

10

The Place of the Arts

*The most beautiful things in the creating of the child
are his "mistakes." The more a child's work is full of
these individual mistakes the more wonderful it is. And
the more a teacher removes them from the child's work
the duller, more desolate and impersonal it becomes.*

—Franz Cizek

Michael Greenberg published the following insight:

> There are three activities everybody does regardless of culture:
> *make music, decorate things,* and *talk.* Talking, making music,
> and decorating things are the three things that seem to be basi-
> cally hardwired into the brains of everybody, that seem to hap-
> pen in every group no matter how large or how small. The fact
> is that people invent their own languages, no matter how tiny the
> group; all have a very specific way of decorating their pottery or
> their bodies or something—whatever it is they can decorate,
> they decorate; and all have some kind of music that comes out
> of their own experience. To me, this says these are three modes
> of expression that almost tumble out of the human brain unbid-
> den, as it were. They're just part of who we are.[45]

This passage contains an insight of particular significance for education. I
confess to being largely unaware of its import until a few years ago, and I
would probably even now not appreciate how profound it is had I not

been prepared for it by a curious event that took place a few years ago. In the spring of 2000, I addressed the (last) international conference on "Learning in the 21st Century," sponsored by Arthur Andersen. The company at that time was still in possession of its reputation for excellence as auditors and consultants, as well as for being on the cutting edge of education. The audience included participants from all over the world. At the time, a distinguished Indian educator and government official, Dr. Manu Kulkarni, approached me, and expressed his pleasure at what he had heard.

Some months later, I received by mail a book sent from India by Dr. Kulkarni. The inscription said, "Presented to Daniel Greenberg … in appreciation of his radical thoughts on Learning in the 21st century," but the title, *Art: The Basis of Education*,[46] seemed to contradict both the inscription and everything I had been advocating. The whole point of my talk was that no particular subject forms the "basis" of education. I was puzzled that the sender would expect me to welcome a book that appeared to champion a particular subject for instruction.

I laid the book aside. There it would have stayed, except for another accidental occurrence. It appears that Dr. Kulkarni has a relative in New Jersey whom he visits from time to time. In the summer of 2001, he was planning to visit, and he wrote that while he was here he would enjoy getting together. (As it turns out, he never did get an opportunity to come up to Massachusetts.) The prospect of meeting him again face to face, without having anything to say about the book he had kindly sent me, made me scurry to pull it off my shelf and take a look at it. I was in for one of the most pleasant surprises of my life, one that once again illustrated the old dictum, "You can't tell a book from its cover" (or from its title).

As soon as I saw the motto that headed the Preface, I knew that something special awaited me. It said, "The artist is not a special kind of man but every man is a special kind of artist." Imagine, then, my delight when I read in the book such statements as the following:

> If we ignore the inherent nature of children while planning educational programmes, we shall be imposing adult notions and objectives on them, which would mean not allowing them to fully enjoy their childhood in their own world and to grow accordingly. According to Indian folklore, a child taught without taking its instincts into consideration is like a caged parrot which has forgotten its own language, but can go on repeating the words taught to him by his master. The present system of education is

an example of that very phenomenon i.e. teachers trying to turn children into parrots and depriving them of their childhood. … If children were not only allowed but also encouraged to remain in their own world as long as it was necessary for their natural course of development, they would grow into well-fulfilled persons. (pp. 42–43)

When someone learns something, it is not because that person has been taught, but because the person has learnt it himself or herself. … Indeed, there is no such concept as teaching in Indian culture. … [quoting Vinoba Bhave] "In none of the fourteen languages in which the Indian Constitution has been written the word teach exists; but there is a word for *learn*. There is no equivalent of the English verb, *to teach*, in Sanskrit or any of the other Indian languages. … It is the egocentricity of the teacher that he thinks that he can teach. As long as we cherish this pride, we will never be able to understand the essence of education." (pp. 96–97)

Genuine freedom is one of the greatest teachers. (p. 113)

Children are looking for new experiences all the time, and want to examine and put everything to test that attracts their eyes or feelings. … Things that the child gets attracted to are often those which the adults either do not see or are not interested in. In short, there are two different worlds—one is that of the adult and the other of the child. … It is not that the adult is unable to see the things in which the child gets interested. The point to note here is that an item may be the same but its function, even its form and the angle from which it is viewed, will be different from the child's point of view. (pp. 29–30)

But by far the most exciting feature of the book was its mention of "the work done by an Austrian artist named Franz Cizek," which the author described as "revolutionary in the field of children's creativity in practical terms," and which "protected the child from adult domination." I had never heard of Cizek, which it turns out was very much my loss. Devi Prasad's book pays homage to this great pioneer and directed my attention to the book that most extensively discusses Cizek's work and theories, *Child Art*, by Wilhelm Viola.[47] Thanks to Prasad and Viola, I have now been able to revel in the insights that flowed from Cizek's creative mind, and to appreciate one of the great, innovative thinkers in education.[48]

It turns out that Cizek formed a start-up group to found a school in the 1890s, in Vienna, the heart of the Austro-Hungarian empire. Here is how Viola tells the story:

> Cizek came to Vienna [from Leitmeritz, a small town in Bohemia, then Austrian] when he was twenty [in 1885], and entered the Academy of Fine Arts. He lodged with a poor family, where, fortunately, there were children. These children saw him painting and drawing, and they wanted, as Cizek has so often related, "to play painter too." Out of his genuine love for children, one of the reasons of his success, he gave them what they asked for—pencils, brushes, and paints. And beautiful works were created by them. It was a happy coincidence that Cizek was in close contact with the founders of the "Secession" movement, a kind of revolution of young painters and architects against the old academic art. He showed his friends ... the drawings of his children, and these artists were so thrilled that *they encouraged Cizek to open what they scarcely liked only to call a school, but for which they had no other name. There children should be allowed, for the first time, to do what they liked* [emphasis added]. (pp. 11–12)

Needless to say, the authorities did not go for the idea, based as it was on (in Cizek's words) the concept "to let the children grow, develop, and mature." He did, however, manage to open a juvenile art class based on the same principles, which, because it did not depend on government funding, did not suffer from state interference.

Cizek continued to promulgate the radical ideas that arose from his eye-opening experience while still a young art student. Viola's book contains several extraordinary quotes from Cizek's conversations and lectures,[49] some of which deserve to be recalled here:

> "How do you do it?" [asked by his interlocutor, Francesca M. Wilson]

> "But I don't do it. I take off the lid, and other art masters clap the lid on—that's the only difference."

> "But you must show them some things; you must at some time have pointed out to them their mistakes in proportion. Don't you point it out so that the child should learn and improve?"

"But on the contrary. Children have their own laws which they must needs obey. What right have grown-ups to interfere? People should draw as they feel."

Young children usually are more sensible than teachers and parents suppose. Their brains are still fresh, they conceive many things in the shortest time which grown-ups do not understand, for they are too anxious.

And, finally and amazingly, consider this insight of Cizek's into parenting:

There are three types of parents—first, those who are always fussing after their children, controlling and correcting them and trying to make them walk in the same paths as themselves; then the infinitely preferable variety, who neglect their children altogether; and lastly, the ideal kind, who watch their children from a distance and are ready with encouragement and friendship when that is needed. (Viola, p. 35)

Viola's book about Cizek is replete with insight into the role of the "teacher." Here are some of the things he has to say:

You must take the child seriously. He knows at once if you take him seriously or not. But it has no sense—quite apart from the moral side—to simulate.

We should give significance to the child and to the work he creates. This does not mean boundless praise. A lukewarm atmosphere is the right one for a child. Cold, negative criticism is deadly, but extravagant praising is not without danger. In presence of a miracle of beauty in a child's work one feels sometimes one must shout, "It is marvelous what you have done. That's as beautiful as van Gogh or Gauguin." But one uses more modest words. It should be restrained praise, giving the child the feeling that it is quite natural for him to have done such a good picture. Still, if a teacher is rather inclined to take for granted everything good the child does, the danger is greater that he may give too little than too much appreciation.

Paradoxically as it may sound, help as little as possible. The question arises whether the adult should or can help at all. We believe in the indirect method. Sometimes a word will be sufficient, a look, a nod.

Cizek had used art as the point of entry of his thinking into a whole new world of education—an avenue that had never occurred to me. He realized that children by nature are capable of real, indeed often great, art; that artistic activity is natural for them; and that adult interference in the natural development of children as artists was detrimental to that development. From that starting point, he made a leap into the entire realm of education and child development, concluding that the natural, unhindered growth of children enables them to reach their full potential as human beings, and that adult interference in general is more of a liability than an asset in this process of growth. That leap, from art to all domains of maturation, was an intuitive one for Cizek and his followers. It was not until I read the article referred to in the opening paragraph of this section that I not only gained an understanding of the real basis for Cizek's intuitive leap, but I also achieved a new and enriching perspective on the nature of education, one that I had hitherto hardly noticed.

The key is the observation that certain activities are universal, transcultural, and therefore related to the very essence of being a human. Even more significant and telling—and here once again Cizek hit upon the truth, albeit not consciously—is the fact that these same activities are engaged in by children from the earliest age, and therefore are not, indeed cannot be, the products of sociocultural influences. This places these activities in the realm of biological evolution rather than the realm of cultural history.[50] And because these three activities—making music, decorating things, and talking—are the outcome of hundreds of millions of years of evolution, they must represent in and of themselves an important aspect of the exalted place humans occupy in the natural world. In other words, these activities not only represent the outcome of evolution, but they also represent important features that account for the specific place that the *Homo sapiens* species occupies in the natural order.

To allow children—and indeed adults—to engage in these three activities to their heart's desire is to allow them to realize their fullest potential as human beings. External interference in their exercise, although perhaps sometimes justifiable for social reasons (man is, after all, a social animal too, another aspect of evolution), always involves some diminishing of their ability to become what they by nature are inclined to be.

Once this is realized, it is almost impossible to comprehend the enthusiasm with which educators and child development specialists advocate systems for coercing children, against their clear inclination and will, to curtail these activities in favor of an externally imposed adult agenda.

Although there might have been some economic justification for such curtailment in the industrial age, there is no longer the slightest pretext of an advantage gained through the suppression of the natural, evolved behavior of children.

In light of all that has been said, one is hardly surprised to find these three activities dominant in an environment such as that of the Sudbury Valley School: Everywhere you look, you see children talking, listening to or making music, and participating in a variety of artistic enterprises (drawing, painting, photographing, looking at pictures). After reading Prasad/Viola/Cizek, I suddenly noticed the obvious for the first time: The school is a hotbed of activity in the arts. Before I encountered these authors, I had realized that artists seemed to flourish here. After my encounter, and the thinking that ensued, I came to understand that the arts are not just another feature of the school: Instead, they are an integral and central part of the school. As a verbal person, I had grasped that fact much earlier when it came to talking, to making conversation. Now I finally had the whole picture, and the underlying reason was human nature.

Well, not quite the whole picture. There are two other transcultural activities: play and curious exploration. Both of these are engaged in by all people everywhere, and by children from the earliest age. They belong side by side with the three previously listed—making music, decorating, and conversing. That play and curiosity are an essential aspect of human nature, and a key product of biological evolution, has been understood for a long time. Aristotle clearly recognized curiosity as the source of all innovation and creativity, and many observers had commented on the importance of play.

The significance of all five aforementioned activities in the evolutionary scheme can be even more adequately appreciated when one understands that all of them exist, in one form or another, in other species, but that none of them exists at a level of complexity attained in human beings. Other animals play, although only a few continue to do so as adults, and none have developed the panoply of intricate games that people have invented. Other animals communicate using sounds, although none has created languages with syntax, grammar, structure, and vocabulary that even remotely approach that of the most "primitive" human language. Other animals poke around curiously in their surroundings, although none has taken curious exploration to the lengths taken by humans. Other animals make noises of varying pitch and intensity that can certainly be called music, but none compose sonatas or symphonies. Some other animals find ways to adorn themselves, but none with the diverse means of expression developed by humans. These five activities not only are integral to being human, but the extent to which humans have developed them *on their own initiative* shows that evolution has endowed them with special significance as indicators of, and indeed the chief architects of, the dominance of the human race on this planet.

Leadership, too, is an art. It cannot be taught, because it requires talent. Although talent cannot be transmitted from one to another, others can help recognize and develop it. Such recognition and development should be a major objective of education.

The word *art* has at least two related but different meanings. In one, it is virtually synonymous with *skill*, as, for example, when we speak of the art of furniture making or the art involved in architecture. In this sense, the terms *arts* and *crafts* are also almost synonyms. A craft is an activity that produces a product that has artistic (*aesthetic*) qualities, but these are not primary. Their *utility* function is primary. For example, a chair designed by Eames or Saarinen is first a thing on which to sit, and second, a work of art. Similarly, a building is first of all a shelter, and second, in some cases, a work of art. On the other hand, some works of (fine) art have no utility, their primary purpose being aesthetic (for example, a symphony by Beethoven, a painting by Cezanne, a sculpture by Rodin, or a play by Shakespeare).

The division between the fine arts and crafts is not a fine line but a gray area. This is why many art museums also display crafts such as furniture and pottery.

Production of great art and craft works always involve skill, but having the requisite skill is not sufficient; *talent* is also required for greatness. Different fine arts and crafts require different talents as well as skills.

The two functions of aesthetics, as I understand them, are first to *inspire* the pursuit of ideals, its *creative* function. An ideal is an objective that can never be attained but can be continually approached. The second function is to stimulate a disposition to continuously pursue ideals, its *recreative* function. The recreative function provides pleasure in the pursuit itself. It provides "the pause that refreshes." Without such refreshment, continual pursuit of something that can never be obtained is not sustainable.

The recreative function of art is embedded in entertainment. This is why we often refer to entertainers as artists. However, an entertainer is not the same kind of an artist that a Beethoven or a Cezanne was. Lucy and Sinatra entertained, they did not inspire, but Beethoven and Cezanne still do.

One may acquire a skill by practice (for example, by riding a bicycle). Acquisition of a skill can, in some case, be facilitated by instruction. Most people can be taught to draw, and in some cases to do so well. But, there is no way to teach someone how to be a great graphic artist. The skills involved in producing fine art or in producing artistic crafts can be developed from scratch, but not the talents required. Although talent cannot be taught, it can be nurtured and developed.

Most people, young or old, have some kind of talent, artistic or otherwise. However, few have many different artistic talents. (Michelangelo and da Vinci were exceptions.) For example, a great composer might not be able to produce a great painting or vice versa. Therefore, one of the most important functions of education at all levels is to enable individuals to discover what talent or talents they have and, once discovered, to learn how to develop it or them.

A talent can only be discovered through practice. (Written examinations cannot do it.) For example, we can only find out if we have a talent for painting or writing by painting or writing. Therefore, effective education should provide "students" of all ages with opportunities to explore a wide range of arts and crafts and, thus, enable them to find out for which ones they have a talent.

The effective uncovering of talent cannot be directed by others; only by self-direction. However, it can be facilitated and enhanced by others. Artistic standards should never be externally imposed on learners. Where they are, great artists such as van Gogh go undiscovered for much too long. Most great artists go unappreciated by those who set and preserve standards of quality in art. Breaking rules is an essential part of artistic creation. The initial presentation of great works of art—for example, Stravinsky's *Firebird* and James Joyce's *Finnegan's Wake*—have even created overt hostile rejections by audiences. Even when great artists form a "school," as the impressionists did, each individual member is unique and produces works whose creator can easily be identified by the work.

A vision of an ideal, or approximation to it, attracts and mobilizes followers who are willing to pursue that vision even if it requires personal sacrifices to do so. The ability to *articulate* a vision is also a requirement of *leadership*. A leader need not be the author of a mobilizing vision, only the articulator of it. And a leader must be able to do so in such a way as to attract followers by inspiring them. Robert Hutchins formulated Mortimer Adler's vision. Hutchins was the leader, not Adler. Followers are attracted to a vision because it is one they share even if they have not been able to articulate it as well as the leader has. Articulation of an inspiring vision is a work of art and is an essential part of leadership.

A leader must also be able to articulate a strategy for pursuing the vision, a way that promises the possibility of progress toward realization of the vision. Fine artists do not necessarily have this ability, but leaders must have it. For example, van Gogh certainly produced a new vision of what painting could be; but he was hardly a leader. Some attract followers by example. Innovators are often imitated but they do not lead.

Without the requisite talents—to articulate an inspiring vision and a strategy for pursuing it effectively—one cannot become a leader. Therefore, most so-called leadership-development programs are shams; they make a false promise: to make leaders out of managers or administrators. They are based on the failure to distinguish between administrators, managers, and leaders

Administrators are ones who direct others in the pursuit of *ends* by the use of *means*, both of which have been specified by a third party. For example, one who supervises a group of clerks who perform a routine task such as order entry or preparation of purchase orders is normally an administrator. What his or her subordinates do has been specified by an authority higher than their immediate boss, the supervisor. In general, supervisors are administrators. Government is full of administrators because the bureaucracy of which they are part usually specifies the ends and means to be employed by those who must do the actual work.

A manager is one who directs others in the pursuit of ends by the use of means that the *manager* selects. Many who are called managers, even in the private sector, are really administrators. The more autocratic an organization, the fewer managers and more administrators. The more democratic an organization, the more managers and fewer administrators.

A leader is one who directs others in the pursuit of ends by the use of means that those he leads select, in the sense that those who follow a leader do so voluntarily. Those who are followed involuntarily, because they can exercise authority over the followers by punishing them for noncompliance, are commanders. A commander is a type of manager, not a leader. For example, Joan of Arc was a leader, because she could exercise no authority over her followers. But General Patton was a commander, a military manager, not a leader. He ruled by authority.

Leadership is *a practice*, not a subject, as these were previously defined. As a practice as well as an art, leadership cannot be taught. If the requisite talent is present, leadership can be developed, but not without it. As a practice, it is best learned either through self-motivated explorations or through apprenticeship with one who has and can demonstrate the requisite talent and skills.

Schools—preschool and kindergarten through universities—can nurture leadership where the requisite talent exists, but they cannot produce it. They can help identify and develop the necessary skills and thereby improve the quality of management. This is equally true of continuing post-school, adult education. Nurturing leadership requires providing opportunities for the requisite talent to reveal itself, recognizing it when it does, and helping talent (and the skills that must accompany it) to develop.

Possession of the skills required by the crafts or the fine arts can contribute significantly to the quality of life one can achieve. They can become the core ability involved in one's vocation or avocation. Use of these skills in either way can enrich life, and this is what education should be about.

PART 3

Envisioning Ideal Lifelong Education

The rule for every man is, not to depend on the education which other men have prepared for him—not even to consent to it; but to strive to see things as they are, and to be himself as he is. Defeat lies in self-surrender.

—Woodrow Wilson

11

Why, and How, We Should Be Envisioning an Ideal Educational Environment

I can prove at any time that my education tried to make another person out of me than the one I became. It is for the harm, therefore, that my educators could have done me in accordance with their intentions that I reproach them; I demand from their hands the person I now am, and since they cannot give him to me, I make of my reproach and laughter a drumbeat sounding in the world beyond.

—Franz Kafka

We have tried to show that current educational systems require transformation into systems that enable people to learn how to learn effectively and to be motivated to do so throughout their lives. Such a transformation requires articulation of a vision of what the system ought to be.

The process of idealized redesign has been described in the following terms:

An idealized redesign of a system is a design of the system with which its designers would replace the existing system right now if they were free to replace it with any system they wanted.

Therefore, the designers begin with the assumption that the current system was destroyed last night, but that its environment remains exactly the same.[51]

In the same spirit, the practitioners of idealized design describe three requirements that should be satisfied in such a process:

- The system designed must be *technologically feasible.* It must not incorporate any technology that is not currently available—no science fiction.

- Although the design need not be capable of being implemented now or later, it must be *operationally viable*—that is, capable of surviving in what would be its environment if it were to come into existence now.

- The system designed must be *capable of being improved continuously* from within and without—that is, capable of rapid and effective learning and adaptation—an ideal-seeking system.

Those involved in the redesign process must know what they would do if they could do whatever they wanted. Such knowledge is essential if they are to set meaningful goals for the future.

The outcome of such a design is idealized in the sense that the resulting system is ideal seeking, not ideal. It should be subject to continuous improvement with further experience and changing environments. The only certainty is that some of whatever we think we will want five or ten years from now will not be wanted then.

Such a vision should be inspiring, a work of art. It should facilitate making short-run sacrifices for the sake of longer-run gains. It should provide the holy grail of a crusade to transform the educational practice now in place.[52]

Why redesign the whole system? Why not be satisfied with gradual transformation brought about by fixing some of the individual failings in the existing system one at a time?

The reason is simple: The failings are systemic and not simply a collection of defects that can be whisked away with some simple touch-ups. The failings are all interrelated and stem from a fundamental flaw in the premises underlying the entire current educational paradigm—namely, that the system must be based on external control of the clients it serves, because of their inability to be responsible for their own education in the context of a modern, developed society.

We have set out to develop an idealized design for lifelong education. We have placed before the reader all the key elements in our thinking as we progressed toward our goal. In this spirit, we have included not only our constructive thinking, but also why we believe the major elements of the present educational system need to be replaced—why, indeed, we can conceive of a new system based on the assumption that the current one was destroyed last night.

The context of this book is a developed Western liberal democratic culture in general and the social environment of America in particular. The process of envisioning ideal education for other cultural settings is certainly important for the betterment of those who inhabit such settings. However, we have chosen to focus our efforts on the setting within which we have grown up and functioned all our lives and with which we are most familiar.

This we shall set out to do in this part of the book.

12

The Preschool Years

The passion for lifelong learning—tireless, all-embracing, persistent learning—manifests itself in every person from the moment of birth. Ideally, during the early years, children should have the opportunity to explore the world around them freely; they should be allowed to figure out, in their own way and at their own pace, how to handle the objects and people they come into contact with so that they can fashion for themselves a model of reality that will develop in scope and in depth as they proceed through life.

The common view is that children are rather passive creatures at birth and, unless there is constant active stimulation by adults, they will not develop properly. This view is also widely held to be true for older children, even adolescents. What it amounts to is a belief that the human animal is static by nature and might stay put at any particular state of development at which it has been left alone; that action is needed on the part of adults to bring out a child's potential for development, which she is not capable of realizing on her own.

However, anyone who observes children closely soon comes to the conclusion that they cannot grow up and master the world quickly enough. Nature endows them with the innate drive to become adults. A child knows all too well the gulf that exists between himself and grown-ups, and is eager to bridge that gulf to reach the adult levels of achievement that he sees all around him. Indeed, only an enormous effort can *stop* a child from realizing her tremendous drive to grow and mature. This drive is a fundamental characteristic of young animals that is essential to the survival of species throughout the living world.

It is during the early years that human beings engage in the most intense and comprehensive learning of their entire lives—and virtually all of it is self-initiated and self-motivated, with little help from adults who act as "teachers." The preschool child is the ultimate autodidact in a staggering range of endeavors.

Just compare, for example, a newborn baby with a 2-year-old toddler. The former has yet to learn to interpret the inputs of his senses, to control his muscular actions, to develop balance and proprioception, to relate or communicate with other people, or even to understand that he exists as an independent being. The latter has come a long way in learning all of these things, and has done so despite starting out with little but her own innate abilities, and despite facing repeated failure along the way.

Few people stop to consider how incredibly difficult these task are to master. Learning how to crawl, for example, is a monumental achievement. The movement of all four limbs has to be controlled and, more important, coordinated, to achieve a goal that has to be recognized. This process can be followed by any observant parent. It begins by the infant consciously desiring to move herself toward an object she desires to touch. Slowly the arms and legs come into play, in no predetermined pattern. At times, uncoordinated movement yields no overall change of position whatsoever. At times, the legs alone come into play or the arms alone. Often, the movement is retrograde, and she finds herself farther from her goal rather than nearer. Other times, she discovers that her actions have flipped her over on her back, from which she does not know how to recover. (Soon, flipping over and back again become goals in themselves.) Yet, she persists; she slowly gets better at what she has set out to do, she solves a host of problems on the way, she overcomes obstacles with grim determination—and she finds herself, at long last, an accomplished crawler.

This kind of complex learning takes place throughout the preschool years. It can be seen very early when a child learns to bring objects to his mouth by using his hands. It can be seen later when he laboriously learns how to stand erect and walk. Perhaps most spectacularly, it can be seen in the prolonged and painful process of learning speech.

To speak, ever so many factors come into play. The sound of the word has to be distinguished from the ambient noise. The child has to realize that this sound has significance and has to conceptualize the notion that it serves to relate what goes on in his world to what goes on in another person's world. He has to grasp the concept of "symbol"—and understand that this word-sound is a symbol for something that he has experienced.

He has to figure out that the other person to whom he is relating is using that symbol to represent experiences, too. Indeed, he has to become aware that he and the other person are similar beings and somehow have similar experiences that can be compared.

All this is not as hard as figuring out what precisely the word symbolizes. This is a philosophical problem first examined in depth by Socrates some 2,500 years ago and reexamined by an impressive array of profound thinkers to this day. In fact, it is no closer to being resolved today than it has been in the past. The child, like the adults around her, has to be satisfied with makeshift, ever-changing definitions of words and has to be able to use words effectively throughout life.

One stands in awe of the tremendous learning ability of the preschool child, never surpassed in later years. These abilities are used to the fullest in the child's insatiable thirst to grow up and become a functioning adult. They accompany her at all times as she grows up and enable her to engage comfortably and naturally in self-motivated lifelong learning.

We have seen many ways that society attempts to curb children's self-directed activity and to replace this with adult-controlled behavior. The approach we have been advocating is to promote the desirable end that every person will develop in his or her own individual manner as completely as possible. From our point of view, not only is it nature's scheme that each child strives to mature in a unique manner, but it is also our obligation to do everything we can do to encourage this to happen and not try to replace the child's striving with ours.

The first major consequence of this point of view is that children's development is enhanced by filling their needs, to the extent that one can ascertain them and that children can express those needs. Many people think that children are "spoiled" if their needs are fulfilled. However, if it is true that children want to grow up more than anything else, it follows that the needs they express service that drive and that satisfying these needs hastens the maturation process—indeed, makes it possible.

The reason so many people say that satisfying children's needs makes them more demanding and more dependent is that most parenting practices deflect children's real needs and attempt to substitute for these the parents' conception of what the needs *ought* to be. Children are taken off their own path toward independence and maturation and placed on a path of adult creation, which necessarily makes them dependent on adults all the time, if only to find out where they ought to be headed.

Consider feeding. When an infant expresses a need for food, that need should be met, whether it is a short or a long time from the last feeding. In the long run, that's the way to maximize the child's independence. The child, as part of integrating herself into the family, will eventually learn to modify her self-driven routines to adapt to those of the people around her. By contrast, most people think that it is necessary to put children on a schedule so that they can be fit into the life patterns of the rest of the family, and so they can get used to the fact that they cannot "have their way" all the time. In this manner, people create an artificial eating pattern for the child that the adult world has decided is for the child's benefit in growing up. As a result, children learn to eat not when they really want to, but when the parents want them to eat. That's step one, which deflects children from recognizing their own internal regulatory mechanisms and teaches them to depend on an external mechanism to decide when they're going to eat.

Now let's consider the next step: spoiling. When children are on a schedule, the tendency is to accentuate the difference between how they are treated at feeding times and how they are treated during the intervals. In the intervals, they may be allowed to cry or be alone—essentially, some form of punishment is meted out for not conforming. But come feeding time, they are held and caressed and fussed over. The artificial need that has been created is overindulged, sugar-coated. This is a pattern that is seen over and over again with children: Parents—or other adults in authority—deflect them from the needs that are really there, substitute something the adults want them to desire, and then overindulge the substitute. This makes the children more dependent than ever on the adults because they haven't gotten what they really want, and they become more and more desperate to get the substitute so that they can, at least, have that and not be totally deprived. This process creates thoroughly dependent people who are "spoiled" in the sense that they are dependent on things that they don't identify as essential according to their own inner compass and look outside themselves to identify what others think ought to be essential.

When discussing an infant's needs, there is a danger in underestimating what goes on in her mind. Many people believe that infants are pretty much "out of it," that they do not have much understanding of anything. These people are always amazed when they discover through some experience that an infant does, in fact, comprehend this or that. It is always fascinating to discover—usually by some accidental observation—how much sense infants make of their surroundings. It is rare that adults get a chance to see this, and one needs to observe children long, hard, and most carefully, but every now and then one is rewarded with insights into how a given child has seen certain patterns in the surroundings, and has followed them, understood them, and responded to them.

It is really very difficult to get any kind of picture of what is taking place in an infant's mind. It is necessary to be extremely sensitive, and try to read the signals as carefully and accurately as possible. More important, it is necessary to learn to live with the realization that most of what is going on will be missed. This is perhaps poignant, but it is neither tragic nor damaging. If everything possible is being done to meet a child's needs, and he is relatively secure, he will come to know that even though he hasn't gotten his message through to his adult caretakers, it is not for want of an effort on his part. In that way, a child learns from the outset of life how to deal with the frustrations and disappointments that are part of everyone's existence, young and old.

What it all comes down to is simply this: The basic problem with infants is communication. They exist in a world of their own, replete with sensations, emotions, feelings, and understanding. But, they have not yet figured out how to relate to the outside world, in particular how to communicate with other human beings. In general, we can distinguish three phases of human development that are determined by the communication problem. The first phase is infancy, from birth to about age 1. This is characterized by losing one battle after another to get through. Infants have all kinds of ways to get attention but really do not understand what the world is about; nor do adults understand what their world is about. Both sides are struggling to understand each other, with the infants struggling much harder because of their inherent drive to mature.

The second phase extends from around ages 1 to 4. This is the period during which the child slowly develops mastery of the surrounding adult language. Children begin to feel their oats, learning to communicate, gaining an enormously detailed worldview but still being terribly frustrated much of the time because their ability to communicate lags so far behind their understanding. The third phase is the rest of life, when, in effect, people have mastered the art of communication and can articulate what they have on their mind. Generally, their understanding, and their ability to communicate their understanding, are rather well matched.

The difficulty in communication is what makes the first year or so of life so important to all that follows. During that year, children don't have adequate mechanisms to process the information they receive, they don't have the verbal apparatus to summarize their experiences concisely in words, and they have a limited ability to access their memory to retrieve stored information. This means that the things that happen to infants during that first year, although influencing their future behavior, are not readily accessible to later review and analysis. This is a potentially dangerous situation: Infants are persons to whom significant experiences happen that are often beyond their ability to process and that can leave a permanent impact on their development for the rest of their lives. What an enormous burden this places on the adults who are responsible for an infant! By contrast, with an adult, experiences can be processed and stored in memory in such a way that they can later be recovered, reprocessed, re-analyzed, and reintegrated into the adult's worldview. Adults are capable of dealing with their environment and adapting to all sorts of life experiences. They go through disappointments, failures, successes, and dangerous encounters; and throughout all these things their character remains fairly constant. Not so the infant, for whom most experiences are mostly irretrievable.

This is why external intervention in an infant's self-initiated development is potentially much more dangerous than with an older child. One can explain things to older children and can help integrate their experience into their understanding of life. For a preverbal child, intervention represents raw power, a blatant suppression of initiative. This is why adults should try to be especially tolerant in the first year, putting up with things that will not necessarily be put up with later. It is part of healthy development for children to learn from their own experience that they can't do this or that. It is generally a negative experience any time a child learns that external forces have to be acceded to, without understanding why.

The most important single thing for children to learn is to be independent, to learn about themselves and their environment on their own. Setbacks may get them mad and frustrated, and they will probably express their anger with gusto, but that's something to be encouraged. It is good for them to be the prime movers and to be able to express freely their reactions to their various experiences.

Of course, parents are responsible for keeping their children safe from physical harm. (In general, adults are ethically bound to do their best to prevent another person from imminent physical danger.) What constitutes a dangerous situation is a matter of judgment. Children do not willingly subject themselves to hazards they are aware of, and they learn from trial and error to avoid dangers that are not catastrophic. Parents thus walk a fine line between allowing their children to discover for themselves what to avoid while still keeping their children from doing irreversible bodily harm to themselves by engaging a severe hazard with which they are not familiar.

The years from 1 to 4 constitute a transition period for the growing child, during which the child is developing the means of effectively interacting with the outside world, both verbally and nonverbally. This period can be seen as a "first adolescence," because adolescence means a period when a transition takes place to a more advanced stage of development. Modern Western culture has limited adolescence to a later period associated with puberty, but in fact an earlier adolescence occurs between the ages of 1 and 4.

During this period, many of the fundamental relationships and attitudes toward the rest of the world are determined, in a manner quite different from the first year of life. The way children are treated in the first year essentially determines how secure they will be, how confident in themselves. These are internal characteristics, largely focused on their personal psychological development. In the period 1 to 4, at issue are the child's basic attitudes to other people and to the rest of the world. Those are the years when they are developing their powers of interaction, and what is critically important is how others will respond.

This has many implications. Suppose a child is struggling to get across something. It won't take him long to find out whether anyone is paying attention, making an effort to understand his imperfect communication. Children brought up by parents who did not take enormous pains to understand them during ages 1 to 4 are going to conclude that their parents don't really care about them, don't really have time for them, and aren't really sensitive to what they need (typical adolescent complaints). The parents might have been concerned about their children's physical comfort, might even have given them all the security and warmth they needed during the first year, but this still doesn't make up for what happens from 1 to 4.

Not only is the attitude toward parents largely set during that period but also the attitude toward much of the adult world. Children who are surrounded by other adults or older children who pay attention to them, and who try to understand them, tend to develop a positive view of humanity (and the notion that it is possible to do something with themselves). By contrast, children that age who are placed in an indifferent surrounding are likely to come out with a pessimistic attitude toward the world—that it just does not pay even to try, because others aren't going to listen anyway. By the time such children reach age 4, they are likely as not to be full-blown cynics. This might sound odd, but a 4-year-old cynic is probably the norm in Western culture. It doesn't take much observation of children to verify that view. Most young children are cynical about conducting any meaningful communications outside their peer groups. This is the root of the so-called generation gap; it is between ages 1 and 4 that it all begins, and that is when the main effort has to be made to prevent this from happening.

The developing communication system of children encompasses not only their interactions with parents and other people but also their interactions with the world around them. Children aged 1 to 4 who are given the opportunity to relate freely with the outside world, and to master it, are likely to develop a constructive attitude toward the world. They must be allowed to putter around, to play with tools, to experiment, and to handle food and pots and pans in the kitchen. They must be allowed to make mistakes, and to spill things sometimes, to waste occasionally, to break a few things. Children know they are making mistakes when this happens; they are not under any illusions. Children are perceptive, down to the finest detail. It is a tremendous error to think that children cannot concentrate on detail. Quite the opposite: Children have a fantastic ability to focus on minutiae, and they get terribly upset when every little thing isn't just right. When a child spills some flour, there is no doubt that a mistake has been made. If that is allowed to happen, children get the idea that making mistakes is a normal and a healthy thing, and nobody is going to hurt them for it. Eventually, they will get the feeling that the physical environment is something that they can cope with. In contrast, children who are partially isolated from their physical environment—not allowed to mess up the kitchen, not allowed to go out and get dirty, not allowed this and not allowed that—grow up to be afraid of machines, afraid of nature, afraid of going out of doors, afraid of the rain, afraid of everything. Overprotecting children turns them into strangers within their environment.

Many people hesitate to give their child sufficient freedom because they fear the waste that this entails, and the expense. One day the child is into tissues, the next day toilet paper, the next day flour, the next day something else, and so it goes. It also appears as if she is bent on destroying everything.

In this situation, a little patience and perspective goes a long way. First, it becomes obvious after a while that children are not out to destroy but rather out to learn how to handle their environment safely and properly—the exact opposite of destructiveness. In the process of learning, they make mistakes, just as adults do when they get into something new. Let children alone, and before long they will be comfortable with everything, and waste will stop. Restrict them, and they will be increasingly frustrated and angry, and the seeds will have been sown for real destructiveness.

An additional factor comes into play in a significant way at this age and continues to be important through childhood: adult role modeling. All children look to adults to learn social behavior, or at least to try to imitate social behavior that the adults around them consider to be appropriate. The importance of positive adult role models in a child's life cannot be overstated. This is true regardless of social status. Rich children can be as deprived in this regard as children who languish in extreme economic and cultural poverty. Where parents, or close caretakers, are not able to serve as role models for their children, society owes it to itself to make up for this deficiency if it wants children to grow up to make positive contributions to their community as adults.

It is crucial to get things right during this age span because by the time the child matures, basic attitudes have set. To be sure, anything can be reversed later in life—nothing is absolutely final. However, the enormous effort that it takes to reverse an attitude set by age 4 is much, much greater in every respect—time, concentration, failure rate, money—than the effort that it takes to raise free-range children from 1 to 4. Of course, it is not easy always picking up the pieces after such children. It seems so much simpler to have a little robot who can be put into a playpen or a controlled area and just left there unattended. But the time spent during those years is paid back in spades during all the rest of life, because the result is a person who feels nurtured and is at home in her environment.

Another issue during the preschool years is dependency. During the first year of life, children are completely dependent on their parents and on the adults around them for everything; without care, they would perish because they don't have the mobility, the knowledge, or the physical coordination to satisfy their basic needs. Children age 1 to 4 are in an adolescent transition between dependency and independence. They're ferociously trying to become independent but, in fact, they are to a large extent still dependent, and that's a source of a lot of problems for children and parents. On the children's side, the problem is that nothing is more irritating to a person who wants to be independent than to be dependent. It's simply humiliating and galling, at any age. This is especially the case with growing children, because children are focusing their whole existence on the drive to mature and to become independent. Every little instance of dependence infuriates them.

As a result, children during that age are often given to attacks of frustration and anger, which are directed more at themselves and their inability to do what they want to do than at any other person. It's not that adults have to be tolerant of unacceptable behavior. Instead, it's a matter of realizing that such outbursts are an integral part of the maturation process. If children were never angry, they would never engage in the difficult struggle to become independent of your nurturing and help. Setting boundaries for children's behavior is walking a tightrope between crushing their initiative and teaching them not to interfere with the lives of others with whom they interact.

For children to develop in a healthy manner during the preschool years, the adults around them—and in particular, their parents—need an enormous amount of patience. In the last analysis, the way a society treats children during these years determines whether it will treasure creativity, curiosity, and mutual respect in the adults these children will become.

13

A New Look at Schools K–12

From our discussion, it can be seen that the ideal environment for people to become educated should have the following characteristics:

- **Learning takes place through self-motivation and self-regulation.** People should be able to learn what they are eager to learn, on their own initiative, and what they are ready to work hard at. They should be free to choose their sources, their materials, and where they feel a need, their teachers. It should be a setting in which students are independent and are treated as responsible human beings.

- **Equal status is given to all interests.** The idea that one activity, or one subject, is inherently superior or preferable to another—the basis of all predetermined curricula—has no place in such an environment. All areas of investigation should be considered equally valid, with no hierarchy of subjects.

- **The output of learners is judged through self-evaluation, a concept that includes the freedom to seek outside feedback.** They should be encouraged to seek feedback from, and provide feedback to, their fellow colleagues. More often than not, students accept positive and negative feedback from other students willingly and apply it to self-improvement. In addition, in providing feedback to other students, they themselves usually learn more about the subject at hand. There should be no tests or grades imposed by outside authorities. This feature alone guarantees the flourishing of individuality and creativity in the learning environment.

- **Learning groups form based on common interests.** They should not be formed based on age, pre-assigned groupings, or preconceived notions of what the best sizes are for such groups. This ensures, among other things, a predominance of age-mixed groupings, such as take place all the time in the world of work and play, with all the consequent benefits of age-mixing.[53]

- **No artificial distinction is drawn between learners and teachers.** All can learn, and all can teach, depending on the circumstances.

- **All members of the learning community participate fully in regulating its activities.** The community should operate as a participatory democracy, as befits an educational environment in a liberal democratic environment. The community as a whole should be responsible for all aspects of its functioning—making rules, enforcing rules (through a fair judicial system established and run by the community), managing the finances, and determining who should be employed and what their duties should be.

These characteristics are key elements of an ideal learning environment. They apply with equal validity to schools for children in the typical K–12 age range and to schools established for older students (colleges, graduate schools, technical and vocational schools, institutions for specialized study, centers for research and instruction, and so on). Indeed, these characteristics applied to many places of learning for adults in times past. In recent times, socioeconomic factors that we have discussed at length have caused children to be treated as incapable persons requiring constant guidance and supervision. Because there is no reason to continue to do so, it is past time to begin the process of change that will transform current educational settings to environments more closely approaching the ideal.

What would a school having these characteristics look like? What would it be like if students of all ages initiated their own activities, created their own environments, and took responsibility for seeking whatever help they needed from adults?

We would expect such a place to teem with activity. Children doing what they have chosen to do will proceed with great intensity and concentration. Some may be reading, some talking, some playing. Some may be working in the darkroom developing or printing photos. Others may be in a dance class, a history seminar, or in the woodshop. Some may be making music, and others studying French, biology, or algebra. Children may be at computers, doing administrative work in the school office, playing chess, rehearsing a show, or participating in role-playing games. A group may be selling food that they made to raise money for new equipment. Elsewhere, they may be found drawing, painting, sewing, or working in clay. Always, there are people playing happily and busily, indoors and outdoors, in all seasons and all weather.

The school could contain rooms with designated functions—for example, quiet reading, drawing, woodworking, computers—each furnished with the necessary equipment. There is outdoor space for games and self-organized play, and there might be an indoor gymnasium fully equipped for gymnastics, exercise, and games. For events, and for the schoolwide meetings that govern the school, there would be a room large enough to hold all school personnel at one time.

The school should be open all day, allowing students to arrive and leave when they want (as long as they fulfill state-mandated attendance requirements). Because there is no predetermined scheduling, students are free to spend as much time on any activity as they want and to move between activities when they want to do so. Schedules of special events are posted and announced.

The ease with which children of all ages, and adults, communicate with each other will be strikingly noticeable. Such a school is permeated with an atmosphere of comfort, self-confidence, and bustle. Given the freedom to fail without censure, students will often challenge themselves to work hardest on their weaknesses.

Although there is no set curriculum, such a school will develop in students many valuable tools that will prove useful to them as adults in the modern world. They will learn how to concentrate and persevere. They will learn how to ponder ethical questions. They will learn to ask for what they want, and strive to get it. They will learn how to try something and relish success, and how to try something and fail at it—and try again. Above all, they will learn how to know themselves.

In addition, students at such a school will be well prepared to function as citizens in a democratic society. Because the school operates as a participating democracy, every student and teacher has an equal voice in all decisions, great and small. Policies about behavior, use of facilities, expenditures, staff hiring, and judicial procedures are all determined by discussion and decision making in a democratic legislature.

The school, in short, is a place where freedom is cherished, where mutual respect is the norm, where children and adults are comfortable with each other, and where learning is integrated into life at all times.

In fact, several schools exist today that possess these characteristics for children ages 4 through high school age. They have been functioning for more than 80 years. The experiences of children in such schools, and their subsequent lives as adults, have been richly documented.[54] The flavor of such schools is wonderfully conveyed by the words of a graduate who spent his entire school life in Sudbury Valley School:[55]

> I didn't really *think* about getting an education. I didn't understand the idea of having to artificially "get" an education. I thought that you lived in the world, and you got smarter because every day you were learning. I thought that there was no way to get dumber unless you were erasing stuff out of your brain! It seemed to me that one day you were talking to someone about one subject, and another day you were talking to someone about another, and that eventually you'd get around to all of them.

> Outsiders would ask, "What did you learn today?" And we'd think, "What did we learn today? What are you talking about?" Because it wasn't as if you went into the library and learned your facts for the day. You had a dozen conversations with people. We weren't learning subject by subject. We were learning in a much more organic manner. You would be doing a lot of different things, and you would learn them in little bits and pieces that would start adding up to much bigger pictures. You wouldn't really know where it came from a lot of the time. By the time you were done learning about something, information was coming from so many different sources—from books and from people you were talking to, and from a long drawn out experience—that you had no idea how you learned it.

14

The College and University Experience

Universities have become extensions of the traditional high school, and post-school education has become an extension of university education. All the failings we have discussed earlier apply as much to universities as to K–12 schools. The student experience in college is no more supportive of their individual development, creativity, curiosity, eagerness to learn, and acquisition of collaborative learning skills than was their earlier experience.

College appears to be serving the primary social function of keeping young people out of the workplace for an additional four years and enabling them to continue to exist without the need to participate as full members of the larger adult society. The extent to which this is true can be gauged from the intensity with which college is being promoted as an essential prerequisite to entering the job market successfully. High school graduates are being told that failure to go to college will set them back in the workplace and reduce their lifelong ability to earn a living. Indeed, pressure is mounting in educational circles to provide free college education to anyone who desires one. We seem to be headed for the same kind of transition that took place during the twentieth century, when entitlement to a free education was extended from elementary school through high school.

Colleges and universities are also serving another social function: to provide employment for many of their graduates. This is consistent with the growing trend of expanding government-funded agencies and services, all of which provide jobs and security for the huge numbers of college graduates who need to find environments that do not deviate in their essential characteristics from the school environments in which they have spent 18 or more years, from early childhood onward.

The question that deserves close reexamination is this: Why should we have colleges at all? What is the purpose of an undergraduate "liberal" education, and how does it differ from other forms of post-high school education?

Young people generally leave the high school environment between the ages of 17 and 19. Many high school graduates move directly into the larger, "real" world and go on to lead successful and satisfying lives. This is true not only of those who enter the trades, or pursue careers as artists, but also of many who enter highly sophisticated hi-tech domains. However, although many of them have a clear idea of the careers they want to pursue in the next stage of their lives, a great many, if not most, have not yet finished their process of maturation and are still seeking to understand themselves and their goals in life. For these, it is important to provide an environment in which they can continue to develop, to sample from among the limitless areas of interest available in the world, to learn at their own pace and in their own manner, and perhaps most important, to interact with people, young and old, and expose themselves through conversation and collaboration to the intellects and wisdom of others.

Colleges should focus on areas of intrinsic value to students, studies that are pleasurable to study, not studies of extrinsic value that require practice.[56] The objective of undergraduate education should be to provide an environment that gives a person the opportunity and leisure to enjoy exposure to a wide variety of intellectual and life experiences.

In college, one could study art in order to enjoy it, to appreciate it more. One could delve into literature, or history, or philosophy, or various sciences, for the sheer joy of learning, not necessarily with a career in mind.

Undergraduate education should have another important function. It should foster and encourage *creativity* and continue to enable students to *develop their ability to learn how to learn* and *to be motivated to do so continually* during their lives, for the rewards and pleasure intrinsic in learning.

And, there should be no entrance requirements (only exit, and then only if a student seeks certification of expertise in a field).

Such an environment should provide an ideal surrounding in which these young people can complete their process of maturation, can discover their strengths, weaknesses, inclinations, interests, and ultimately, their destinies. Such an environment is what the undergraduate college should be: open to all who want to experience it and focused on individual realization rather than specific career development. A student who feels ready to leave college is a student who is either ready, finally, to engage the world directly or one who is ready to go on and acquire further expertise in a particular field and become certified to practice in that field.

By contrast, the function of graduate education is the development of practitioners—people adept at practices. Practices are activities that can only be learned by engaging in them. Nevertheless, such learning can be significantly supplemented and consolidated by reading and listening. Examples are the practices of medicine, law, and architecture, and also the practices of teaching or conducting research. It is this characteristic of graduate education that dictates many of the properties it ought to have. It is also this characteristic that differentiates it from undergraduate education.

Practices cannot be taught. They must be learned by engaging in them. Learning through practice cannot be organized into subjects, courses, semesters, and other discrete units, nor can it be coerced or imposed on students.

A graduate program based on practice should take all its stakeholders into account. In the case of medicine, for example, patients, their families, insurers, doctors, nurses, technicians, and service personnel are some of the stakeholders. It is only through engagement in practice that awareness and appreciation of the presence, desires, and needs of all the stakeholders can be acquired.

Practices do not deal with sequences of independent (separable) problems. The problems with which they deal are interrelated, and their solutions are interdependent. Reality consists of sets of interacting problems, systems of problems we call "messes." As previously noted, problems are abstractions extracted from reality by analysis. Therefore, education for practice should develop and apply methodology for dealing holistically with systems of problems. Because messes are complex, this requires an ability to cope with complexity. It is much easier to deal with complexity through design in practice—for example, in designing a skyscraper—than in dealing with it academically in a classroom or research facility. The *theory* of complexity is not required for dealing with complexity in practice; design can handle it.

To avoid turning out graduates from a common mold, there should be no prerequisites for entry into a graduate program. *However, there should be exit requirements,* a demonstration of an ability to practice effectively and responsibly in the chosen field. The variety among incoming students increases the opportunities for their learning from each other, particularly of learning subjects not directly connected to their practice. To increase this variety further, students should design their own educational programs without being constrained by "requirements." They should be able to make use of any source of learning that they want. Their designs should be reviewed by experienced practitioners. A program's faculty should make available to students its opinion as to what information, knowledge, and understanding are required for effective practice in its field, and what is optional but desirable.

Students may or may not use the information provided by the faculty in designing their programs. However, they should be required to defend their choice of activities, subjects, and methods of learning when they submit their designs for review.

Where the practice normally involves recipients of a service (for example, clients), they should be involved in all student practices.[57] Clients should have the right to reject any student trying to serve them. Clients or their surrogates should pay for the services received. This is necessary to make the practice realistic enough to yield a great deal of learning and to ensure that the client is giving the practitioners the support they need. The income generated in this way can be used to contribute to self-support the program and to provide financial support to students.

Research cells can be organized around practice, around engagement in the profession to which the program is devoted. Students can self-organize research cells with one or more faculty members for the purpose of raising to consciousness what they are learning in practice, and for the purpose of learning how to communicate it effectively to others.

Graduate programs should be directed by the students, faculty members, and support personnel together, with each person having one vote (the "Committee of the Whole"). Their approval should be required for selection, retention, and dismissal of a faculty member.

All faculty members in any program should have the same rank and title. This is intended to make each program a classless society. It will also reduce internal political maneuvering that currently occupies much of the time of many on faculties of colleges and universities. Tenure should not be provided to faculty members, because it protects incompetence more than academic freedom. Moreover, reliance on courts established for the purpose could ensure academic freedom more efficiently than tenure.

Rules governing all phases of each program should be established by the Committee of the Whole. The committee should also establish a judicial procedure, involving all components of the graduate program's population, for the purpose of ensuring that the rules are properly and fairly enforced. The judicial procedure should contain explicit provisions for protecting the academic freedom of all members of the graduate program.

In most academic institutions, faculty offices are arranged much like cells for monks. The privacy and inaccessibility of faculty members is maximized. Informal interactions among faculty members and between them and students are minimized. Nevertheless, such informal interactions can be valuable learning experiences for both faculty and students.

Instead, faculty and student facilities should be provided in open spaces where contact with others is very easy. In addition, a variety of small breakout rooms (for small group study or conversations), conference rooms, lounges, rooms housing computers and office equipment, and auditoriums should be part of any graduate facility.

One of us (RLA) had an experience that illustrates the possibilities opened by a radically different approach to graduate education:

> Two students from less-developed countries, Peru and Brazil, came to me one day and asked that the program offer a course on planning for development of less-developed countries. They pointed out that five members of the faculty had done such planning for such countries. The students also said that 13 of them were from less-developed countries, all of whom had expressed interest in such a course. I told the deputation of 2 that we would offer such a course but it would have to be taught by the 13 students.
>
> The students, in a state of shock, asked, "Then who will be the students?" I answered that the five members of the faculty would be. They then said these faculty members already knew a great deal about the subject. Good, I said, then they will have to find out what they knew before they could arrange a course for them.

The students then asked whether they could expect the faculty members to do assignments, attend regularly, and behave as students are normally expected to behave. I assured them the faculty members would be good students as long as the course made their expenditure of time in it worthwhile.

The students asked for a semester to prepare. It was given to them. The course that followed was presented by the 13 students, each talking about development planning in his/her country. It was one of the best courses I ever attended.

The organizer of the course became the chief strategic planner for the World Bank, later followed by a similar role in his home country, Peru. His "deputy" became chief planner for a major state in Brazil. Each of the remaining students became active in development planning in their native countries after their graduation. They had learned enough to do so by teaching, not by being taught.

Perhaps the designation "graduate education" is a poor choice and should be replaced by one that more accurately describes the function of advanced schools designed to produce competent practitioners in various fields. Students who enter such schools would be doing so with the explicit purpose of pursuing a career in their chosen field and obtaining the training, both theoretical and practical, needed to reach an entry-level degree of fitness to practice.

Not enough notice is given to a significant new feature of modern society—namely, that there is now much more opportunity for pursuing multiple careers during one's lifetime, thanks both to the extension of life spans and to the readier access to training facilities. Although lifelong careers will doubtless continue to exist, especially for people with a highly focused sense of calling, we can expect more and more people to undergo several career changes during their lifetime. Therefore, the training schools that prepare for specialized careers can be expected to an ever-increasing extent to find people of widely varying ages applying for entry and certification.

This means that adults who have already pursued a career (or more than one) and want to change to another will turn to these schools, which will thus serve as "retraining" facilities. Albert Schweitzer, who, after performing as one of Europe's leading organists for many years, decided in his mid-30s to become a physician and serve in Africa as a missionary-physician, will no longer be viewed as an exceptional case, but will become an archetype for a more modern career paradigm of shifting interests, preceded by successive waves of specialized education.

The new landscape of education will also allow for young students, recently graduated from high school, to proceed directly to their "graduate education," without undergoing the additional years of maturation and focusing afforded in colleges (or after attending college for only a few years). Once again, there are harbingers of this approach in those schools that allow students to go directly from high school into a multiyear medical program. Such schools and programs are still rare but can be expected to be the norm when the different functions of college and "graduate school" are finally sorted out and differentiated from each other.

15

Education and the Working Life

Because of the rapid development of new knowledge and the rapid obsolescence of the old, adults past school age increasingly experience a desire for further education for one (or both) of two reasons: either to maintain or increase their work-related competence; or to engage in learning for its own sake, as an end in itself, as a source of personal satisfaction. Consider each of these in turn.

Most people in the workplace require occasional "retreading." The percentage of time spent in learning to improve and update performance is bound to grow. Therefore, the distinction between work and learning will become less and less important. Learning will become a part of work, and work a part of learning.

This is reflected in the currently growing interest in knowledge as an organizational resource. Corporations have become major educational institutions. Indeed, it is likely that more education is taking place in corporations than in schools. Educational institutions also provide some of the continuing education that is required, not necessarily on their campus, but much of it at places of work or educational facilities that noneducational organizations run.

The main drawback with the current practice is that it treats people with extensive experience much like naïve beginning students and derives little, if any, advantage from their experience. Such education should be conceptualized in a very different way than that for students not yet practicing in the real world.

Those attending continuing-education programs should be active contributors to the program, not passive recipients of information and knowledge. They should have abundant opportunity to exchange what they know with others attending. They should be able to compare notes on what they know and believe they need to learn.

The materials presented to them in classes should always integrate a "so what" discussion and examples of relevant applications of what has been presented. Nothing is as convincing to those attending such courses as successful applications of what is presented to them. Supplemental visits to places at which such applications have been made can prove particularly worthwhile.

Universities, vocational and technical schools, and businesses should offer "competence-maintenance programs" in selected areas to subscribers who want to stay up-to-date in a designated field. These programs would continuously survey developments in the designated areas and report them regularly along with a list of sources for the acquisition of more detail. Such programs are already being offered on the Internet in a spontaneous manner. With the passage of time, we can anticipate that more of these will be sponsored by individual specialists or groups organized for this purpose.

Learning for its own sake, not work related but basically recreational, can be expected to expand in coming decades. Here, too, the Internet plays a crucial central role. High-speed connections, combined with sophisticated computer programs, will put an ever-growing number of individuals in contact with each other, and with the accumulated wisdom and knowledge of human culture. In addition, colleges and universities should, where possible, expand access to their offerings to adults who have completed their schooling, without imposing admission requirements. Such access is currently given in evening or daytime extension programs, as well as in those that are located in a variety of settings— museums, libraries, community centers, and religious institutions.

A highly effective way of learning new things and being stimulated to do so is through discussion. It is through discussion that one becomes aware of what one thinks about a subject or issue, and what others think about what one thinks. Therefore, people should be given opportunities to form small groups, "learning cells," which can meet to discuss topics they have selected. Readings or other material may be distributed in advance to serve as a focus of the discussion to follow. Visitors, including experts, can be invited to present materials to the group or to express their opinions about the topic up for discussion. The sessions can be informal and may be combined with lunches (even brown-bag lunches) or evening sessions in members' homes.

With time, each member will become aware of the interests of other members of the cell. They will be eager to bring to the attention of others in the group any material they think would be of interest to them. There is no better way of being kept up-to-date in any field than by having others dedicated to keeping one informed of relevant developments.

Corporations, nonprofit organizations, research institutes, and other goal-oriented institutions also have considerable incentives to encourage educational endeavors other than those devoted to training for specific skills. Unfortunately, all too often this has been considered irrelevant to the main institutional mission. A company devoted to manufacturing something, or providing certain services, tends to be committed to focusing directly on its primary function, without "wasting time or money" on extraneous, seemingly frivolous activities.

The modern socioeconomic situation has radically altered workplace reality. The mobility of workers, both skilled and unskilled, has made it easier for people to transfer from place to place and from job to job. Now more than ever, keeping a functioning team together necessitates finding ways to make employees at every level satisfied with their conditions. In addition, rapid and continuous changes in every domain of human activity require every institution to be flexible, to be responsive to changes in the cultural environment, and above all, to be creative. What can be more effective than cultivating a more nurturing, and understanding, environment for all employees, one in which people are comfortable, feel valued and empowered, and feel appreciated as individuals?

This is the reason we hear more every day, from organizations seeking to acquire or retain employees, about offers of childcare, fitness facilities, and other such amenities, as well as of a variety of health and retirement benefits. Of increasing significance will be the availability of opportunities for learning and for free communication.

Because most employees are willing and able to set their own agendas for exploration and learning, they should be given ample access to up-to-date means of communication and information retrieval. Space should be provided for informal meetings, and quiet rooms for reading and study. They should be encouraged to invite experts for discussion and exchange ideas in fields not directly related to their daily work.

An interesting phenomenon is at work relative to both work-related continuous learning and learning for its own sake. The easier it becomes for people to gain access to sources of learning, the greater the demand for such access. CDs, DVDs, the Internet, multimedia person-to-person interactions, cheap and easily available hard-copy printed material—all contribute to the public demand for more: for better quality, more relevance, and greater depth of information, knowledge, understanding, and wisdom. Supply creates demand. We can anticipate a time when practically everybody is both a learner and a facilitator of learning, accessible to anyone else. In such an environment, the surrounding culture becomes a source for lifelong continuing education from which anyone can benefit.

16

Taking "Retire" Out of Retirement

The industrial era wreaked havoc on both ends of the age range. Just as children were excluded from active participation in the life of the community, so too, older people were shunted aside, out of the mainstream of society. Where age had been revered as a repository of accumulated wisdom, it now came to be regarded as a symbol of obsolescence contributing little of worth to a society or its culture.

The post-industrial milieu has rendered moot all the reasons put forth for this unfortunate treatment of what we now call "senior citizens." Because of continually increasing life expectancy, there is no longer any upper limit to the age at which a person can participate fully in the intellectual and productive life of the community. This is true due to two significant developments.

The first of these is the spectacular increase in the speed and accessibility of information exchange and retrieval. This has made it feasible in principle for people everywhere to tie into limitless opportunities for learning, human interaction, and personal growth. All the educational modes we discussed in Chapter 15, "Education and the Working Life," apply not only to people in the workplace, but also to people of any age after they have completed their formal schooling. In fact, nothing we said there is characterized by any upper age limit.

The second development has to do with the changing nature of the modern economic scene. With each passing year, there are fewer barriers to the creation of new niches in the economy, which enable people to be productive, to meet newly identified desires and needs, and to generate income.[58] In addition, businesses, schools, universities, professional groups, the trades, research institutions, and nonprofit charitable organizations are finding that the experience of older citizens is an invaluable resource, and that it is highly worthwhile for them to tap into this resource.

There is no longer any need to "retire" when you reach what is commonly referred to as "retirement age." Indeed, it is likely that the concept of retirement age, which did not exist for most all of human history, will become a relic of a quaint era, looked at by future generations as an oddity that existed for a few hundred years in so-called developed economies.

Lifelong learning is the key to this welcome advance in the human condition—or, perhaps more properly stated, this welcome return to an age-old practice of treasuring old age! By making no age distinctions in the availability of educational opportunities, there no longer have to be age distinctions in the degree of incorporation of people into the social fabric.

PART 4

Excursus:
Funding Ideal Schools

Ideal schools will differ according to the needs and desires of their constituents. They all, however, would share some key characteristics. All are devoted to encouraging the maximal possible realization of each student's aspirations. All provide an environment in which students define their own goals, are activated by self-motivation to work toward realizing their goals, and are given free reign to learn (on their own and with the collaboration of others) in such manner and at such pace as they wish. All are self-governing communities where all stakeholders have a full voice in determining all aspects of their operation—rules, finances, personnel, and administration.

Ideal schools represent a decentralization of education, and the devolution of the responsibility for each person's education to that person throughout life. The greater community—the nation, the state—obligates itself, constitutionally, to provide support to each individual's lifelong quest, and to finance that quest during each person's youth. The extent of "youth" is an evolving concept. Initially, when state-supported mass schooling came into being, it was provided free of charge for 6 years, usually beginning at age 6 or 7. Currently, the trend is to extend the beginning age for state-financed education downward, to 3 or 4 years old, and there is much talk of extending it upward beyond the prevailing 12 years of elementary, middle, and high school through 4 or more years of post–high school study for those who want it.[59]

Up until now, state-financed education has brought with it state-controlled education. The state, and during the past generation the federal government as well, have inserted themselves directly into the detailed operation of all schools, in matters ranging from curriculum, to testing, to teacher qualifications, to defining special needs, to facilities, and so forth. The range of activities wherein local school districts can exercise discretion has been greatly narrowed, and freedom of action for individual public schools has been all but eliminated. Even private schools, hitherto allowed considerable latitude, are increasingly coming under governmental control.

The ideal schools discussed in this book are based on the premise that each school is a self-governing community, with limitations imposed solely by the collective decisions of the community, and by the realities imposed by the outside world.[60] But removing state, or other outside, control over the educational functions of these schools does not remove the state's constitutional obligation to support each individual child's education. The question, ever so important to the implementation of ideal schools, is this: How can these schools be funded by the state and yet retain the autonomy that they require to function?

The key to the answer is the notion of "vouchers," which has been discussed in various forms for several decades. We believe that a voucher system designed along the following lines will provide adequate support to ideal schools and will meet many of the objections raised to voucher systems that have hitherto been proposed:

- **Who gets a voucher?** The parents or guardians of each school-age child (the "bearer" of the voucher) will receive a voucher annually for each child; the voucher will be given directly to children who have reached the age of majority.[61]

- **What is the value of a voucher?** When the system is first installed, a voucher will be worth the average cost per student, averaged over the ten school districts of the state having the highest average cost per student.[62] This ensures that, from the outset, the quality of education available to every child will not be subject to the criticism that the state has been offering inadequate funding to support the program.

- **What can be done with the vouchers?** Parents can use these vouchers to pay for a child's admission to any school of their choice that admits them (see ahead). In particular, any group of parents can join forces and use these vouchers to create a school for their children, as long as the school is not affiliated with a religious organization or does not provide religious instruction.[63]

- **What reporting requirements will be placed on schools?** Any school receiving vouchered students will be required to prepare financial statements that conform to accepted accounting standards and are available to the public. In addition, every such school will be required to make public the framework of its educational program, and how this framework translates into action.[64]

- **How will schools be financed?** There are two aspects to school financing: operating expenses and capital expenses. Public schools will be distinguished from private schools as follows: For public schools, vouchers will provide the only source of income for the operation of each school. (This means, among other things, that schools that either cannot attract sufficient students to be viable, or cannot find mechanisms to keep their expenses under control, will not survive.) Private schools, however, will be able to charge tuition greater than the value of a voucher. Parents of the students admitted must make up the difference.[65]

Every school will be responsible for managing its own operating budget, *in toto*. This means that each school will control, among other things, the number of teachers and staff that it will hire and the salaries being paid to them. Expenses that often are capitalized by accountants will generally be considered part of the operating budget—for example, the acquisition of office equipment or computers.

As for capital expenses directly related to plant costs, each school, when first established, will have to negotiate with the existing local and state authorities for the acquisition of physical plants. In many instances, conversion of the school system to a decentralized collection of ideal schools will involve provisions for transferring existing school buildings to one or more of the newly formed schools. In general, however, capital expenses that incur additional spending on the part of the government—either through direct subsidy or through the issuance of school bonds—will have to be determined at various levels of government or through referendum by the citizenry as a whole.

■ **What school admission requirements will apply to children bearing vouchers?** Parents and children should be free to choose the school with which they want to associate. Schools, in turn, should in principle accept every child who wishes to attend. However, three exceptions apply:

If a school's program requires special skills or abilities from students (such as would be the case, for example, in a school devoted primarily to enable children to focus on their skills as dancers), admission may be limited to applicants who meet the minimum requirements set by the program. If more children who meet the requirements apply than can be accommodated, entry should be by lot.[66]

If the physical plant of a given school does not permit acceptance of all students who wish to attend, admission to the available spaces should be by lot. The capacity of a given physical plant should be decided jointly by governmental authorities concerned with the safety of buildings and the school's needs for space as defined by their program.

■ **What about the cost of travel to and from school?** It has become widely accepted that public schools must provide for the transportation of all students to and from school, provided they live farther than a specified distance from the school they attend. This, the relevant governmental authorities will continue to do, through whatever mechanism they determine will be most efficient and cost-effective.

■ **What about students with special needs?** Any decent society will take care of those unfortunate children who need special attention due to deficits that are no fault of theirs. An educational system consisting of ideal schools will necessarily include schools for children with special needs and provide vouchers having a value sufficient to pay for the services these children need.

This has, however, become a thorny problem in the educational environment that prevails today. The sudden explosion in the number of children identified as having special needs can be directly traced to the cooperative actions of several groups whose self-interest is served, under current conditions, by continually increasing this number.

Thus, because "special-needs students" are either exempted from standardized tests or provided for outside the regular framework for such tests, teachers and administrators whose reputations, financial support, and salaries depend on good test results have a direct interest in removing from the regular test population any students who tend to perform poorly or be in any way disruptive to class discipline. This is done by labeling such students as having special needs, and creating an ever-growing list of "learning disabilities" to justify that label.

In addition, because special-needs students require a large number and wide variety of specialized professionals to deal with them—such as psychologists, tutors, various teaching specialists, therapists, social workers, and physicians—any increase in the number of such students results in increased employment opportunities for people in those various fields. This, in turn, creates demand for more programs to train such people, and so forth. Pharmaceutical companies also have a major interest in developing "medications" to "cure" or "alleviate" the various types of learning disabilities that have been defined.

As long as the people who identify special-needs students are the same people as benefit from their growing numbers, society will have no solution to the increasing costs such labeling incurs. These costs are not only financial, in the form of highly expensive services, but also—and primarily—*human,* in that they undermine the self-confidence and destroy the self-image of a significant portion of the children going through our schools. Society will pay a terrible, and growing, price in human potential if it continues to allow this widespread degradation of so many of its children.

Funding ideal schools through vouchers may well be the only way such schools will ever come into being and be allowed to evolve and learn from their mistakes. Centralized control is ill-suited to the encouragement of innovation and creative solutions. The idealized designs we have been discussing, at their very core, free schools from centralized control of their operations. Vouchers free them from centralized control of their finances, an essential step to completing the decentralization of education required to turn the vision of ideal schools into reality.

Appendix

Sudbury Valley School
www.sudval.org

Founding the School

Envisioning an ideal school was the task before the founders of Sudbury Valley School. Beginning in 1965, they began to design an educational environment from first principles, to examine what education is and how it best takes place. The members of the group came from a wide variety of backgrounds—academia, public and private schools, the professional world, trades, the arts, and homemaking. Few had known each other before they embarked on the project; they connected through normal avenues of networking. They had been driven to participate in the project by a variety of reasons: Some had children approaching school age and were not willing to enroll them in a traditional school setting; others had been teaching in traditional schools and were aware of many of the failings discussed in this book; yet others had reflected on their own schooling and concluded that it had served them poorly.[67]

Everyone had a commitment to some of the same basic principles: that learning does not depend on teaching, but rather on the self-motivated curiosity and self-initiated actions of the learner; that all people are learners by nature, and that children are the most diligent and effective learners; that an environment in which children are expected to grow up to be effective citizens in a liberal democracy must itself be a democratic environment, in which children enjoy the same rights as adults; and that a school embodying such an environment cannot contain within it pockets of arbitrary authoritarianism. These principles have been extensively discussed in the body of this book.[68]

It was a fortunate accident of fate that the school was founded in Massachusetts, in the town of Framingham. Massachusetts delegates to local school authorities the responsibility for approving private schools in their town or city; thus, unlike the situation in most states, no central state government control is exercised over private schools. This situation allows for a potentially highly diverse collection of idiosyncratic private schools, each with their own set of goals and methods of operation.

Founding a school depends, therefore, on two key factors: the ability of the founders to articulate a clear mission and the skill of the founders in conveying the value of that mission to local school officials. Because the population of any private school consists of children whose families voluntarily enroll them in their programs, local authorities are generally supportive of new private school initiatives: It is not in their interest to generate friction with a segment of the local population that wishes to be stakeholders in a new venture.

Sudbury Valley's founders put a great deal of effort into both of these activities: articulating the school's philosophy and vision, through writings, media, public lectures, and small group meetings; and cultivating the cooperation of local authorities in allowing the school to commence operation in 1968.

The greatest challenge the school has had to face from the outset is finding a way to bridge the gap—indeed, the chasm—between what the school has articulated and what outsiders (such as prospective enrollees and their parents) have understood the school to be. Because the kind of school represented by Sudbury Valley, and described as an ideal in this book, differs so radically from the generally accepted kinds of institutions that are currently called "schools," virtually every word used by Sudbury Valley in describing itself has been open to misinterpretation by the public. For example, such a seemingly simple phrase as "freedom to choose whatever activities the student wishes to engage in" is more often that not taken to mean "freedom to choose from a varied offering of classes—those classes that the student elects to take." Most people cannot imagine that the word *activities* might include such unorthodox, un-school-like activities such as play, conversation, looking at TV, video games, hiking, riding unicycles, and so forth. One can hardly blame them, given the virtual monopoly that traditional educational methods have on the practice of "education."[69]

Nevertheless, there has been a marked increase in the number of people throughout the world who are being exposed to the workings of Sudbury Valley. Publications of the Sudbury Valley School Press have been translated into many languages. Since the early 1990s, a number of schools operating along similar lines have been founded in the United States and abroad, in such varied locations as Australia, Belgium, Canada,

Denmark, Germany, Israel, Japan, and The Netherlands, and the number of groups working on founding such schools has been increasing from year to year.

The Way It Is

How do principles get put into practice? Mimsy Sadofsky, a staff member at the school and one of the four founders still working there after four decades, put into words the following image of the school:[70]

> What is the school like? First, let me set the stage. The school enrolls students from the age of 4 up. No one is too old, although most of our students are 19 or younger. The people in the school, no matter what age they are, are each doing what they want to do. Usually that means that some people are doing things with others, who can be of the most various of ages, and some people are doing things alone. Usually it means that most people are doing things not done in most other schools, and some are doing things that are done in other schools with a very unusual intensity and concentration. It more often means that children are teaching adults than that adults are teaching children, but most often people are learning and unconscious that "learning" is taking place. Doing what they choose to do is the common theme; learning is the by-product. It is first and foremost a place where students are free to follow their inner dictates. They are free to do what we all do when we have the time to, and what we all find to be most satisfactory—they play. Play is the most serious pursuit at Sudbury Valley. Some people play at games, and some play at things we who have more traditional educations are more comfortable with—writing or art or mathematics or music. But we are quite clear at Sudbury Valley that it is doing what you want to that counts! We have no curriculum and place no value on one pursuit over another. The reason that we are secure in feeling this way is that we constantly see that people play more and more sophisticated "games," explore more and more deeply, that they constantly expand their knowledge of the world, and their ability to handle themselves in it.

> Children who play constantly do not draw an artificial line between work and play. In fact, you could say that they are working constantly if you did not see the joy in the place, a joy most usually identified with the pursuit of avocations.

I would like to talk about some of the other aspects of an atmosphere that encourages individuality to such an extent.

The school is teeming with activity. The rooms are small and large, many are special-purpose rooms, like shops and labs, but most are furnished like rather shabby living or dining rooms in homes: lots of sofas, easy chairs, and tables. Lots of people sitting around talking, reading, and playing games. On an average rainy day—quite different from a beautiful suddenly snowy day, or a warm spring or fall day—most people are inside. But there will also be more than a few who are outside in the rain, and later will come in dripping and trying the patience of the few people inside who think the school should perhaps be a "dry zone." There may be people in the photo lab developing or printing pictures they have taken. There may be a karate class, or just some people playing on mats in the dance room. Someone may be building a bookshelf or fashioning chain mail armor and discussing medieval history. There are almost certainly a few people, either together or separate, making music of one kind or another, and others listening to music of one kind or another. You will find adults in groups that include kids, or maybe just talking with one student. It would be most unusual if there were not people playing a computer game somewhere, or chess; a few people doing some of the school's administrative work in the office—while others hang around just enjoying the atmosphere of an office where interesting people are always making things happen; there will be people engaged in role-playing games; other people may be rehearsing a play—it might be original, it might be a classic. They may intend production or just momentary amusement. People will be trading stickers and trading lunches. There will probably be people selling things. If you are lucky, someone will be selling cookies they baked at home and brought in to earn money. Sometimes groups of kids have cooked something to sell to raise money for an activity—perhaps they need to buy a new kiln, or want to go on a trip. An intense conversation will probably be in progress in the smoking area, and others in other places. A group in the kitchen may be cooking—maybe pizza or apple pie. Always, either in the art room or in any one of many other places, people will be drawing. In the art room they might also be sewing, or painting, and some are quite likely to be working with clay, either on the wheel or by hand. Always there are groups talking, and always there are people quietly reading here and there.

One of the things most adults notice first about Sudbury Valley is the ease of communication. People, no matter what their age, look right at each other, and treat each other with tremendous consideration and easy respect. Fear is absent. There is a comfortable air of self-confidence, the confidence normal to people pursuing the goals they set themselves. Things are almost never quiet, and there is (to an outsider) an exhausting intensity, but the activity is not chaotic or frenetic. Visitors speak of a feeling of a certain order, even though it is clearly a place full of enthusiasm.

The students at Sudbury Valley are "doin' what comes natur'ly." But they are not necessarily choosing what comes easily. A close look discovers that everyone is challenging themselves; that every kid is acutely aware of their own weaknesses and strengths, and extremely likely to be working hardest on their weaknesses. If their weaknesses are social, they are very unlikely to be stuck away in a quiet room with a book. And if athletics are hard, they are likely to be outdoors playing basketball. Along with the ebullient good spirits, there is an underlying seriousness—even the 6 year olds know that they, and only they, are responsible for their education. They have been given the gift of tremendous trust, and they understand that this gift is as big a responsibility as it is a delight. They are acutely aware that very young people are not given this much freedom or this much responsibility almost anywhere in the world. But growing up shouldering this responsibility makes for a very early confidence in your own abilities—you get, as one graduate says, a "track record." Self-motivation is never even a question. That's all there is. An ex-student has described some of these effects:

> There are a lot of things about Sudbury Valley that I think are on a personal level, that build your character, things that perhaps enable you to learn better, that public school students never have a chance to achieve. When you're responsible for your own time, and spend it the way that you want to, you tend to put a lot more enthusiasm into what you do, instead of being a lethargic lump that's molded and prodded into a certain direction. And when you end up

the way you want to end up, you know you've been responsible for it. It's a lot more rewarding, I think, than when you end up the way somebody else wants you to end up.

Who are the kids in this school? Are they chosen for creativity, intelligence, or perhaps some other standard? It is a private school—does that mean it appeals to only the well-to-do? Admission is on a first-come, first-served basis, and we have never been full. That means that the students in this school consist of everyone who wants to come whose parents will allow them to. It includes the cerebral and the super-active, the "regular" and the "zeroed-in," the full gamut of possibilities. Most of the families who choose to send their children to SVS are looking for something they wish they could find in public schools, but cannot: simple freedom for their children to develop according to their own timetables and their own desires.

Is it perfection? Hardly. But it is tremendously stimulating and exciting.

Sudbury Valley is a functioning democracy. There is a School Meeting that meets once a week to take care of all the management work, either by directly accomplishing it or by delegating it. Each student and each staff member has one vote, and the meetings are run in an extremely orderly fashion. The School Meeting makes a budget each year, ever so carefully, because the tuition is low and it is important to be thrifty and not to spend money needlessly. Yes, kids know this, and are much harsher judges of what is—or is not—a necessary expense.[71] The School Meeting passes every rule, often after weeks of soul-searching debate. This includes the rule about "no littering," the rules about not ever setting a foot in the pond, the rules that govern which rooms eating is okay in, and which ones you can play the radio in, as well as the rules protecting individual rights. It is up to the School Meeting to approve groups organizing to pursue special interests that want budgets or space. Anyone who thinks that young children are not wise about these matters need only attend a few such School Meetings.

The School Meeting delegates some tasks to subgroups or to people elected by them to carry out certain responsibilities. All of us are totally accountable and totally aware of our accountability every minute. The School Meeting also debates candidates for staff, votes on them in an all day, school-wide, secret balloting, and awards contracts according to needs determined by this balloting. There is no tenure.

There is also a subgroup of the School Meeting set up to deal with rule infractions. It is called the Judicial Committee, and its function is to investigate written complaints about possible rule violations, and to see that justice is served, being constantly careful about due process. Does it work? You bet it does. Peer justice is amazingly effective. Rules are often broken, but the culprits are usually good-natured about both admitting what has happened and accepting their punishment.

We have no curriculum. If you send your children to this school, however, there are some certainties about what they learn. They learn how to debate, and how to ask for what they want, and see to it that they get it. They learn to ponder ethical questions. They learn how to concentrate: they can focus on things the way few adults that I know can, and this gives results. The same focus that a 5 year old puts into sand castles a 7 year old puts into drawing, an 11 year old into making a gingerbread house, a 9 year old into chess, a 12 year old into Dungeons and Dragons, an 8 year old into climbing 40 feet up in the beech tree, a 15 year old into writing a story, a 17 year old into making armor, or an 18 year old into preparing for graduation. That kind of preparation will serve them well in each and every pursuit they choose as adults.

[A few years ago there was] a group of about eight or nine young men, aged about 12 up to 19, who have been working together and alone for periods of time up to two years building chain mail armor. It is a perfect example of what happens at SVS. No adult in the school inspired them, and in fact no adult in the school helped them. They have created vests, helmets, and gloves. What they start with is a spool of wire. They must take it and turn it into thousands of tiny open circles, by wrapping it carefully around a thin metal dowel, or several dowels of various thinness, and cutting the coil into many open circles. Then with pliers and infinite patience, they weave the circles into beautiful garments, often using gold wire to weave in designs. They know a lot about history, but they also know a lot about how to determine an interest and follow it, about how to work long and hard for a goal that may not mean a thing to anyone else but enriches the person who is striving for it.

A lot of people think that this sort of school will need tremendous numbers of adults running around making sure that each student's needs are met and easing the way for everyone. In practice this is just the opposite of what we need. Everyone is a teacher and everyone is a self-educator. Mostly what kids need from adults is very little instruction, but willing guidance toward their expressed needs. They want older people around who are successful in the world and who have interests and activities that afford them satisfaction, and pursue them with dedication. What the kids at Sudbury Valley School seem to look for in staff is depth of character; they want people who have looked into themselves and can listen and understand when kids go through the same processes. They want older and more experienced friends to turn to, whether they are older students or adults. They want to have resources to turn to but not to feel obligated to use any particular resources. In other words, wisdom is at a premium. The adults are the people with the larger worldviews to turn to as yours expands.

How does this education end? There is no magic moment when it is over; the idea that permeates the school is that you are a learner every day of your life. But at some time most students begin to feel that they want to move on to a different kind of situation. Perhaps they want to try their wings at living independently. Perhaps they want to continue to pursue their interests in an institution, such as a university, where there is a larger group of people interested in the same area as they are. Perhaps they are ready for an apprenticeship in the larger community, or perhaps they have honed a skill to such a point already that they are ready to pursue it full time. They may leave school to travel the world on a shoestring, or to become professional chefs, or to study fashion design, or to work hard to break into the music business.

Many who leave to go on to the next step in their lives leave with excitement, but most leave reluctantly, too. Among the things they do not take with them are grades, transcripts, evaluations, or lists of courses completed. What they do take is a firm conviction that they can do what they set out to do. We have found that Sudbury Valley students have what it takes to do very well. They have become used to working hard. They are used to working independently. They are used to overcoming difficulties. And they know who they are. They can describe their own strengths and weaknesses and their own methods for exploiting the strengths and overcoming the weaknesses. So they seem to be quite successful in their next pursuits. They get into the colleges they want to go to. Part of that is the process by which they decide to go to college. It is always to pursue an interest they are committed to, and they choose colleges where their interests will be met. But, part of it is the impression they make when they interview. Each one has to talk their way in the door. Because they have spent years and years talking and arguing and thinking about real issues, they are an amazingly articulate group.

Why is such a wonderful school not the norm? Shouldn't SVS already have been copied in a million different places? The answer isn't so simple—or maybe it is. The idea of total freedom for children is very threatening to most people. The kinds of objections that are raised are these: "But there are some basics—how do you ensure that each child learns them?" We at Sudbury Valley are not so certain that there are any basics, but we are certain that our students are in an environment that is real, that is totally linked to the larger community, and that if there are things everyone should learn, the kids in the school surely know it as well as the adults, and it is up to them to ensure that they learn it. Often, people are angry when they learn that most students can learn all of basic math in just 20 hours of classroom work. They feel cheated because they spent years and years of doing repetitive mathematics either because they hated it and weren't interested and were bad at it or because they learned it fast but were told they had to redrill, redrill and redrill some more or they would forget everything. Now I ask you, would you really forget it if it were truly basic?

But what these people really mean is, "If kids are not controlled by rigid authorities, won't they be out of control?" That is the *Lord of the Flies* objection: that children that are free will turn swiftly into cruel creatures. But our children are not in a hostile, terminally stressful environment; they are free in an orderly, rule-respecting society. Yes, they are free to change the rules, but only when they convince everyone else the changes are wise. They are free, and surrounded by models of the way people behave who wish to maintain all their freedoms.

Working Toward an Ideal

It was clear to the founders, and has been clear during the four decades of the school's existence, that Sudbury Valley is a work in progress, striving at all times to approach the ideal conditions it has envisioned. This is an unending process; it shows itself in the school's unfailing resolve to reexamine virtually every action it takes in light of its basic principles, and to attempt to remove inconsistencies that prevent its principles from being realized.[72]

Some examples might be helpful. When the school first opened, the importance of play in all aspects of learning (for adults as well as for children) was barely appreciated, although play was freely engaged in by students from the beginning. The richness of play, its depth, its centrality to the creative process, its relationship to joy and to the pursuit of meaning, all were gradually revealed with the passage of time. Developmental psychology has only recently begun to explore play in greater depth, but even now schools similar to Sudbury Valley remain the only living laboratories for the observation of children given the freedom to engage in play to their heart's content.

So, too, the role of conversation, especially free-flowing, wide-ranging conversation, in enhancing and enabling learning to take place became ever more evident with the passage of time. One wonders how something so obvious from everyday experience could have eluded so many people so long—especially people devoted to the education of children and adults. Similar considerations apply to the invaluable contribution of age mixing, a factor first noticed (albeit in limited context) by the Russian psychologist Lev Vygotsky, but only marginally acknowledged in the realm of schooling.

The atmosphere that prevails in Sudbury-model schools is unique in many respects.[73] It is vibrant, alive, and overflowing with intensity and enthusiasm. The empowerment embodied in the egalitarian participatory democracy of the school—empowerment that makes no distinctions of age, from the youngest 4 year olds to the oldest members of the staff—translates into self-confidence, lack of fear of failure, and willingness to take risks and test new waters. The equal voice given to all stakeholders becomes a shared responsibility for all aspects of the school's operation and survival, from the establishment of rules governing behavior to the operation of a peer-driven judicial system for investigating and evaluating allegations of infractions.

The following reminiscences of a person who attended Sudbury Valley School from the age of 4 until graduation give a particularly rich picture of the atmosphere at school, and of the way students internalized the school's goals:

> We had our own little world. I just remember the atmosphere: big challenges. Every day we had challenges to meet. Maybe today I've got to get better at going around the building, or something like that. Things I was really afraid of, and working on. And a group of us would be working on them at the same time.

> We were so busy. We picked hard things to do most of the time. At Sudbury Valley, there were always older kids who had done things that the younger group was trying to get to. You automatically wanted to be one of the people who could do it, too, so you kept trying until you could do it. Everything was always, "You have to get one step further." I don't know why. Something naturally makes you want to try. It was never stagnant. Everything was a challenge.

> And it was never boring. I've never been bored a day in my life. I was so busy at Sudbury Valley! People often wonder whether the older kids who had graduated and came back to visit helped us know what life was going to be like. The answer is a simple, "No." We were in life. We didn't think about life as "going to be like."

> People talk about their childhood: I had a great childhood. When I was 11, I wanted to stay 11 forever. I was having a great time. People talk about never having had a chance to do what they wanted to do: I did what I wanted to do for 18 years. And I don't have a chip on my shoulder that I never got to do what I wanted to do. So many people I know have that chip on their shoulder.

For years, I heard that Sudbury Valley teaches you responsibility. And I could talk about it in beautiful sentences that would make you believe that I understood what I was talking about. "Sudbury Valley teaches you responsibility by giving you the freedom to be responsible for yourself and by setting standards that have to be met, like the social laws." And then one day, I must have been 9 or 10, a light went off in my mind and I understood what the word *responsibility* meant. I had used it like a name, like my name. *Responsibility* was a name that you used in describing the school. Then I finally understood what that word meant, and it was a celebration for me. "Oh, my God, that's what they mean by *responsibility!*" I had been exercising responsibility, but I didn't realize that the word meant what I was doing. I guess I must have found out what it meant by thinking about that explanation that we give people, and how it actually plays itself out. And one day I got it!

That's what you do learn at school. We used to toe the line because you can't blame anybody else. It's the hardest thing about the school. It's not hard when you're a child, because kids are like that. Little kids want to be responsible for themselves. When you're 6, you know what you want. You want to absorb the world, you want to be busy, you want to do things. You don't want to jump over the same ravine you did the day before!

But it's hard when you're an adolescent, when you're not very happy with yourself and you're struggling for an identity. You want to blame other people for what you don't like about yourself. You don't exactly know in which direction to go, so having the responsibility to choose for yourself makes you angry, causes anxiety.

Kids who went to the school from an early age did things without any idea of what they meant, and at some point they kind of jelled for us. For example, kids who come from the outside think the School Meeting is weird. Kids who just live in it think it's normal, but don't quite know what it is. And then it jells. I always felt that it was very equitable. From the age of 4, I definitely knew I had a vote there. I knew it was a meeting where we got together, organized the running of the school, and talked about it and voted on it; a place where judicial problems that weren't solved in the judicial committee were solved, big problems. I certainly went if there were issues that I wanted to deal with. We would campaign for issues we believed in, even when we were 6 or 7.

We voted for staff—that's how they were chosen. Actually, kids vote for those they believe are good staff people, and they take it very seriously. Even 6 year olds. We thought about it, we talked about it, and we cared. We felt we had the right to decide like everybody else. We didn't feel different from the 12 year olds.

I always thought I was grown up. At every age I felt, not grown up, but a whole person; not a little kid or a big kid, just "me." Like, "Of course I'm not 6. I'm just 'me,' a person with a vote." I wasn't a less powerful person than this 15 year old, or adult, and I thought that was normal.[74]

During the four decades of its existence, the school has seen many alumni go out and make a place for themselves in the world. The careers they have chosen span the full range of career types pursued in this country— academicians, tradespeople, professionals, artists, farmers, clerks, managers, entrepreneurs—in a hugely varied number of fields. Two major studies of alumni have appeared, and they describe the richness of the lives of the school's graduates in great depth.[75]

It is impossible, in a brief summary, to do justice to the full richness of these studies, and of the lives of the school's alumni. Nevertheless, perhaps the following excerpts from the interviews of three alumni can at least give an impression of what they are like as a group:

I'm quite happy. My philosophy is that if you're not happy, you're not doing it right. So if I'm ever not happy with something, I change it. It's kind of bending your path to make sure that what you're doing gives you options that you're going to enjoy. So as you're going down that path, you always head toward the directions that will end up giving you those options rather than the ones you don't like. The ones that get you in trouble from past experience, you don't do again. So it's really not a conscious thing so much as something you learn as you go, and you avoid situations and things that you have found, in the past, you really didn't enjoy that much.

I feel like when I decide I'm going to do something, I do it, but it never turns out exactly how you envision it. I had a vision when I was a child of what life was going to be like. I'm 39 now, and it's completely different from that vision. You get to a certain point in your life when you realize that life's not going to turn out exactly the way that you planned it, and that's okay. You don't have complete control over your life and that's part of the fun. I just keep moving on, seeing where it takes me, and enjoying where I am.

I control my life to a huge degree. That's what Sudbury Valley was all about. You could either take charge, or you could sit there; it was all up to you, and you were the only one who really influenced the way your life turned out, the shape your education took. The responsibility was all on your shoulders, and that certainly has paid off for me. Sometimes I want to give it up, sometimes I want to say, "Why me?" But you can't; you have to take responsibility for everything that happens to you that's not created by some unforeseeable outside force.[76]

There is no reason to shrink from undertaking the daunting enterprise of transforming education in America, and throughout the world. Ideal education and lifelong learning, while remaining perfect goals that can never be perfectly realized, are certainly approachable in real-life, self-improving institutions. The conditions of twenty-first-century culture are forcing that transformation to take place even without the willing collaboration of the powers-that-be in the educational world—indeed, for the most part over their stubborn opposition. The cost of this conflict-laden gradualism, in lives ruined and initiatives dulled, cannot be justified or defended. The benefits to global society in hastening the transformation by engaging the active cooperation and collaboration of professional educators, politicians, and business leaders cannot be overstated.

Postscript

We have tried to present a rationale for a fundamental redesign of our national educational system—a design that will produce citizens who can reverse the devolutionary trends in our society today. We have tried to design a system that will produce people who will engage in continuous self-development and exercise responsible and creative citizenship.

Complete realization of an idealized design is seldom possible. What is usually possible is an approximation to it, some close and some far from the design. It may be that, initially, few will be able to implement all the design elements we have described here. However, over time, successively closer approximations are usually possible.

Although our design is ideal seeking, every aspect of it has been used successfully, just not yet at the scale that meets the national need. We have written this book in the hope that it will encourage and facilitate the scaling up.

We hope the readers are stimulated as much in reading it as we have been in writing it.

Endnotes

1. During recorded history, the "schools" we know about consisted of places where people of all ages, primarily adults, interacted through discourse and sought to understand their world by seeking answers to their questions. Such schools were common in ancient Greece and Palestine and spread throughout the Roman and Persian empires, later developing into the universities of early modern Europe.

2. No one was more aware of the conflicting values of personal liberty and an industrial culture than Thomas Jefferson, for whom the American ideal required that America reject the encroachment of industry on its predominantly agrarian economy.

3. Frederick W. Taylor, *Principles of Scientific Management* (New York: Harper & Brothers, 1911).

4. My own experience provided me with an excellent introduction to the validity of this observation. I was pulled out of the first semester of graduate work by World War II. While in the service for four years, only about six months of which was spent in combat, I worked on my thesis and finished a draft of it by the time I came out. In addition, however, I did one hell of a lot of reading.

   When I returned from World War II in 1946 and enrolled for the usual list of required courses, the graduate chairman called me in and said I was an embarrassment to the faculty because I had read way beyond the content of these courses. He made me an offer. Teach the courses you need for credit, and we'll give you credit for them. I did, and what a learning experience it was! I quickly learned what I did not know, and learned how to consolidate and organize what I did know. They began to give me courses on subjects about which I knew nothing before I started to teach them. What an opportunity! I never did get educated by the department.

5. Motivation is more likely to arise in those who have been read to frequently.

6. "What's Making Us Sick Is an Epidemic of Diagnoses," *New York Times,* January 2, 2007.

7. An example of a healthcare system redesigned along these lines can be found in Sheldon Rovin *et al., An Idealized Design of the U.S. Healthcare System* (Bala Cynwyd, PA: Interact, 1994), pp. 2–5.

8. "Recall that experience is the best teacher. We do not learn by doing things right because we already know how to do them. What we get by so doing is confirmation of what we already know. This has value but it is not learning. We can only learn from mistakes, by identifying them, determining their source, and correcting them. Furthermore, people learn more from their own mistakes than from the successes of others. The great composer Igor Stravinsky put it very effectively: 'I have learned throughout my life as a composer chiefly through my mistakes and pursuits of false assumptions, not by my exposure to founts of wisdom and knowledge.'" Russell Ackoff, "Ongoing Discussion 'Thought Piece'" (Pratt & Whitney Rocketdyne's Enterprise Thinking Network, January 2006), p. 9.

9. "Today we tend toward an almost obsessive fascination with metrics—measurable indicators that can be tracked and used to judge success and failure, progress and decline …. The field of education has … developed increased reliance on metrics and measurement in an effort to raise standards and accountability—with the inevitable consequence that an increasing amount of student time is spent preparing for and taking tests rather than learning. As the old saying goes, 'You don't make a hog any heavier by weighing it repeatedly.'" Eamonn Kelly, *Powerful Times* (Upper Saddle River, NJ: Pearson Education, 2006), p. 51.

10. Jules Henry, *Culture Against Man* (New York: Random House, 1963), p. 288.

11. R. D. Laing, *The Politics of Experience* (New York: Ballantine Books, 1967), pp. 71–72.

12. See the "Appendix" for the discussion concerning Sudbury Valley School.

13. An excellent source for original material on this subject is John Taylor Gatto, *The Underground History of American Education* (New York: Oxford Village Press, 2001).

14. As Alfred North Whitehead put it in his classic speech, "The Aims of Education," the 1916 presidential address to the Mathematical Association of England: "The solution which I am urging is to eradicate the fatal disconnection of subjects which kills the vitality of our modern curriculum. There is only one subject-matter for education, and that is Life in all its manifestations. Instead of this single unity, we offer children—Algebra, from which nothing follows; Geometry, from which nothing follows; Science, from which nothing follows; History, from which nothing follows; a Couple of Languages, never mastered; and lastly, most dreary of all, Literature, represented by plays of Shakespeare, with philological notes and short analyses of plot and character to be in substance committed to memory. Can such a list be said to represent Life, as it is known in the midst of living it? The best that can be said of it is, that it is a rapid table of contents which a deity might run over in his mind while he was thinking of creating a world, and has not yet determined how to put it together." What was true in 1916 is no less true today.

15. The existence of separate departments in universities not only provides opportunities for promulgating professorial influence and affording prestigious positions to protégés, it also solves the unwelcome problem of where to locate someone who has made a mark for himself as an original thinker—at least most of the time. Occasionally, when the problem becomes intractable and the person is widely acclaimed, academia creates the title "University Professor" to indicate its inability to pigeonhole that person.

16. The story is more than likely an urban myth, but its illustrative value in no way depends on its historical veracity. In fact, I experienced something similar in an advanced graduate physics course, where a perfectly correct answer was totally rejected because it did not conform to the explicit traditional format defined by the instructor.

17. C. P. Snow, *The Two Cultures: A Second Look* (New York: Mentor Books, 1964).

18. For a more extensive discussion of these points, see Daniel Greenberg, *Outline of a New Philosophy* (Framingham, MA: Sudbury Valley School Press, 1996).

19. See also Daniel Greenberg, "The Meaning of Play," in *A Clearer View* (Framingham, MA: Sudbury Valley School Press, 2000), pp. 3–30.

20. Frederick W. Taylor, *The Principles of Scientific Management* (New York: Harper & Brothers, 1911).

21. Ivan Pavlov, *Conditioned Reflexes* (Oxford, England: Clarendon Press, 1927).

22. "Children can be taught if we employ the technology needed to teach them. Similarly, children can be motivated if we stop leaving the motivation to chance and engineer the behavioral changes we desire in kids." Siegfried Engelman, *Your Child Can Succeed* (New York: Simon & Schuster, 1985), p. 7.

23. C. Cherry, *On Human Communication* (New York: John Wiley & Sons, 1957).

24. Jonathan Kozol, *The Night Is Dark and I Am Far from Home* (Boston: Houghton Mifflin, 1975) p. 1.

25. Gilbert Highet, *The Immortal Profession* (New York: Weybright and Talley, 1976) p. 1. [Italics in original] Highet recounts an amusing episode, illustrating the lifelong repulsion to school-taught subjects engendered by forced imposition: "A good friend of mine, when I brought out my last book, asked me how many I had written altogether. When I said: 'Fourteen, I think, not counting the little juvenalia,' she laughed, and answered: 'I don't think my Doug has *read* fourteen books since he left school. They shoved *Ivanhoe* and *Silas Marner* down his throat so hard that he still gags when he looks at a bound volume full of print. He never reads anything but the *Wall Street Journal* and *Sports Illustrated.*' Yet her Doug is a capable fellow with a lively and versatile mind. It was early compulsion which 'froze the genial current of his soul.'" (pp. 2–3).

26. "Fresh Faces," *New York Times,* December 8, 1991, p. 50.

27. John Dewey, *The Theory of Inquiry* (New York: Henry Holt and Co., 1938).

28. See the "Appendix" for the discussion concerning Sudbury Valley School.

29. For a comprehensive recent study, see "The Effects of Class Size on Student Achievement: New Evidence from Population Variation," by Caroline M. Hoxby, *Quarterly Journal of Economics,* November 2000, pp. 1239ff. Hoxby concludes, "The estimates indicate that class size does not have a statistically significant effect on student achievement." I rule out even modest effects (2 to 4 percent of a standard deviation in scores for a 10 percent reduction in class size).

30. And those for whom leisure was not available, whose lives were devoted totally to the bare needs of survival, had to focus all their mental and physical energies on the struggle to stay alive. For most of human history, the overwhelming majority of the population fell into this category, and even today, a significant proportion of the world's people remain in this condition.

31. For an extensive discussion of these developments, see Daniel Greenberg, *Outline of a New Philosophy* (Framingham, MA: Sudbury Valley School Press, 1996).

32. One should keep in mind that the basic elements of modern industrialism—the technological know-how, and the physical underpinnings describing the ability of mechanical machines to multiply force and work output—had been in existence from early ancient times. What was missing was the ethical notion that all people might be deserving of the lives that seemed reserved only for the strong and dominant few.

33. It is important to note that during most of the industrial era, education for the leisure elites took a much different form than the schools for the masses. For example, to the extent that elite children were sent to schools at all—and it should be remembered that in many, if not most, cases, education was left to the home environment—the emphasis in the schools was invariably on the impractical, on the imaginative: Latin and Greek, ancient literature, philosophy, and the like.

34. He had the paper in which he developed this theory published in a private printing. Several hundred copies went to Parisian booksellers. None sold. After a while, he went around and bought them all.

35. See, for example, Morris E. Chafetz, *Big Fat Liars: How Politicians, Corporations and the Media Use Science and Statistics to Manipulate the Public* (Nashville: Nelson Current, 2005).

36. It may seem that the lives of people universally excoriated for their evil effects on society are exceptions to this rule. One may argue that Hitler, Stalin, Pol Pot, serial murderers, and others of that ilk are exceptions to the universality of the social aspect of our species. Consider, for example, the following passage taken from a commentary the 24-year-old Mao Tse-tung wrote on Friedrich Paulsen's book, *A System of Ethics:* "I do not agree with the view that to be moral, the motive of one's action has to be benefitting others. Morality does not have to be defined in relation to others …. People like me want to … satisfy our hearts to the full, and in doing so we automatically have the most valuable moral codes. Of course there are people and objects in the world, but they are all there only for me." (Jung Change and Jon Halliday, *Mao: The Unknown Story,* New York: Knopf, 2005, p. 13) An excellent and concise survey of current explanations for the appearance of such people can be found in James Hillman, "The Bad Seed: Eight Explanations," in *The Soul's Code: In Search of Character and Calling,* New York: Warner and Random House, 1997, pp. 227–238).

    People of this sort are actually an extreme example of the rule, not an exception. For them, the nature of their social interaction is rooted in dominance and destruction; the very realization of their destiny requires the existence of a social setting within which their evil designs can be carried out.

37. For an extensive treatment of the development of language in children and its use in social interactions, see Daniel Greenberg, "Children and Grownups: An Essay on Human Behavior" in *Worlds in Creation* (Framingham, MA: Sudbury Valley School Press, 1994), pp. 75–204.

38. In this sense, the contention by such observers as Francis Fukuyama, in *The End of History and the Last Man* (New York:

Avon, 1993), and Natan Sharansky, in *The Case for Democracy* (New York: Public Affairs, 2004), that liberal democracy is the ultimate form of societal organization toward which the human experience evolves, and beyond which nothing further can exist, turns out to be less than adequate. Liberal democracy itself evolves interminably, as the three strands on which it is based are continually being woven into subtler and more refined designs.

39. I consider the situation in such places as equatorial Africa, much of the Middle East and southeast Asia, the Chinese and Siberian interiors, and most far-flung oceanic islands to be parallel to that of medieval Europe, in that they have had some contact with other cultures—they have not been isolated in the manner of some remote jungle tribes—but they have not been assaulted on a daily basis by vast amounts of information the content of which is alien to their native cultures.

40. Institutions that are run democratically have been called "extraordinary organizations"; see www.extraordinaryorganizations.com. Looked at from a slightly different perspective, they have been labeled "chaordic organizations"; see Dee Hock, *Birth of the Chaordic Age* (Berrett-Koehler; 1999).

41. An oft-repeated slogan heard among Jews in Nazi concentration camps during World War II was the word *Ueberleben*—"survival," "making it through another day."

42. The fact that we all are born with the ability to solve problems that face us and develop throughout life ever-more complex and sophisticated techniques to help us solve problems, does not conflict with the existence of many useful methods that wise people have discovered and put to the test for enhancing success in dealing with problems. We have discussed some of these earlier in the book. A particularly useful (and amusing) treatment of this subject can be found in Russell Ackoff, *The Art of Problem Solving* (New York: John Wiley and Sons, 1978).

43. Nevertheless, we hear from educators endless pleas that children have to be "taught how to think" in school. This has a special—and, as it turns out, insidious—meaning: It applies to a specific form of mental analysis called "rational thought," a form invented by the ancient Greeks through centuries of philosophical probing, given its ultimate blessing by Aristotle and

embraced by Western culture as the only legitimate form of thought that can be applied to reality. The term *be reasonable* has become synonymous with *think like a human being ought to think,* and its antithesis, *you are being unreasonable,* is a derogatory term meant to deprive the other person of legitimacy in a discussion.

Yet people thought before the Greeks came on the scene and have always engaged in mental contemplation and worldview formation outside the constructed framework of Greek logical analysis. This is widely recognized throughout the world today; in the West, those who acknowledged this fact were marginalized by the intellectual elites until the middle of the twentieth century, when a strong movement developed in the West to incorporate nonrational modes of thought into the Western mainstream took hold.

It is important to realize the limited nature of rational thought, as well as its usefulness. When one understands that the concept of "how to think" is much broader than the concept "how to think rationally," and is much richer and more useful, and is a natural innate process possessed by all human beings from birth, the need to impose one form of thinking on all children evaporates. To put it another way: Imagine the uproar that would occur if educators suddenly decided that an essential feature of all education is making sure that children know how to think like mystics. Oriental religion and philosophical methodology and Kabbalah would be mandatory subjects drilled into every child, with every subject being embellished by it. Ridiculous? Of course. So is any other attempt to impose a particular form of contemplation on everyone as the primary legitimate way for all people to think.

44. See "Children and Grownups: An Essay on Human Behavior" in *Worlds in Creation* (Framingham, MA: Sudbury Valley School Press, 1994), pp. 75–204.

45. "The Magic of Conversation" (*Sudbury Valley School Journal,* June 2001); reprinted in Michael Greenberg, *The View from Inside* (Framingham, MA: The Sudbury Valley School Press, 2002), p. 23.

46. By Devi Prasad (New Delhi, India: National Book Trust, 1998).

47. Bickley, Kent: University of London Press, 1942. Getting a copy of this book was no easy matter, although it is unquestionably a classic in its field.

48. The others known to me at present were A. S. Neill, whose Summerhill school is well known and whose work dates from the 1920s on; and Lev Tolstoy, whose amazing insights can be read in *Tolstoy on Education: Tolstoy's educational writings 1861-62,* selected and edited by Alan Pinch and Michael Armstrong and translated by Alan Pinch (Rutherford, NJ: Fairleigh Dickinson University Press, 1982)—another book not easy to come by. It is remarkable that the essays on education written by such an eminent author as Tolstoy are not more widely known and read, but perhaps it is understandable that admirers of Tolstoy the author are a bit embarrassed by his radical views on the subject, which are so contrary to the mainstream, as was his experimental school, which unfortunately lasted only a very short time.

49. Cizek himself never completed his projected book, for which he had received funding from Yale University Press; he died before it was completed, and whatever notes or manuscript material he may have developed never saw the light of day. Everything we know of his thoughts comes via the recollections of others. All the quotes are from Chapter IV of Viola's book, *From Talks with Cizek,* pp. 32ff.

50. Here is how Michael Greenberg puts it (*ibid.*): "The rest [that is, other than music, art, and conversation] is up for grabs. Not every culture by a long shot even has writing. …. The rest is technology, so to speak."—that is, the rest is a second-order cultural creation, rather than an inherent human trait.

51. Sheldon Rovin *et al., An Idealized Design of the U.S. Healthcare System* (Bala Cynwyd, PA: Interact, 1994) pp. 2–5.

52. For a brief background overview, see Russell L. Ackoff and Sheldon Rovin, "On the Ethical Use of Power and Political Behavior to Lead Systemic Change," in *Power, Politics, and Ethics in School Districts: Dynamic Leadership for Systemic Change,* edited by Francis M. Duffy, Leading Systemic School Improvement Series, No. 6 (Lanham, MD: Rowman and Littlefield Education, 2006).

53. For a discussion of the effect of free age mixing on learning in such an environment, see Peter Gray and Jay Feldman, "Patterns of age mixing and gender mixing among children and adolescents at an ungraded democratic school," *Merrill-Palmer Quarterly*, 43, 1997, 67–86.

54. See, for example, the ample literature produced by the Sudbury Valley School Press, Framingham, Massachusetts, described at www.sudval.org. This literature pertains in particular to a school founded in 1968 and the group of "Sudbury schools" modeled after it.

55. For a more extensive discussion, see the "Appendix" concerning Sudbury Valley School.

56. As we shall see, those are the focus of what has come to be called "graduate education." Thus, literature and history, for example, would be subjects for college study, but if one wanted to make a career of teaching or doing research in either area, this would qualify as practice and be pursued in an environment—a university—devoted to providing graduate education.

57. Students should not be able to affect clients without supervision.

58. For an extensive discussion of this topic, see the highly readable *The Long Tail: Why the Future of Business Is Selling Less of More,* by Chris Anderson (New York: Hyperion, 2006).

59. Many communities have already made schooling available beyond high school in community colleges that charge minimal tuition.

60. Thus, for example, school communities must obey the general laws of the communities in which they exist and cannot condone activities that violate those laws. Also, graduate schools that train practitioners must interact with client populations in the outside world and see to it that the students they train conform to the requirements professional practitioners in the outside world impose on their profession.

61. The definition of who constitutes a "child"—that is, from what age is a child to be awarded vouchers, and up to what age— must be left to the citizens of each state, who will be footing the bill for the entire program.

62. It is important, in calculating this figure, to include all costs that are typically not shown as part of per-student expenditures in the regular operating budget—for example, contributions made by granting agencies for particular programs and contributions made by governmental authorities (such as insurance or self-insurance, legal fees, and so on).

63. This proviso is essential to preserve the constitutionality of the program. However, general instruction in theology is not prohibited so long as it contains no elements of indoctrination.

64. It can be expected that avenues will rapidly be developed through the Internet for having public feedback on the performance of various schools. Spirited debates on the virtues and vices of various ideal schools will probably be the norm and will greatly help in providing an "open market" for these schools that will be an invaluable tool in ultimately winnowing out the wheat from the chaff.

65. The stakeholders in any school would be free to contribute additional funds out of their pockets toward the operation of that school, if they so wished, or to engage in fund-raising activities to supplement their school's income. It would probably be sensible for most schools receiving vouchers to incorporate as nonprofit charitable organizations and thus qualify for tax-exempt contributions.

66. In particular, private schools that want to accept vouchers must conform to this condition.

67. A detailed account of the founding of the school can be found in *Announcing a New School* (Framingham, MA: Sudbury Valley School Press, 1973, 2007).

68. There has been a considerable literature produced by the Sudbury Valley School Press, discussing various aspects of the school's underlying principles and their realization in practice. For a complete listing, see the "Bookstore" page of the school's website at www.sudval.org.

69. A particularly amusing example of the way young children at school reacted to this dichotomy of meanings is the following reminiscence of a student: "We knew we were in a special place, and we were aware that it was different, but we used to play

'school' at school! Even though we were really busy, we would set aside time to play this game. We would have classes, and we'd have recess, and we would act out images that we heard about public school. Sandra knew about public school; so did Lucia. Sandra and I were the students, and Lucia was the teacher. She actually taught me how to write way before I learned how to read, by tracing letters. I'd copy her handwriting. Maybe the game would last an hour, and then we'd get back to our activities, to our frenetically busy days." Indeed, the founders themselves changed their view of the meaning of the word *play* as they observed the children in the school over the past decades.

70. "A School For Today," in *The Sudbury Valley School Experience, 3rd ed.* (Framingham, MA: Sudbury Valley School Press, 1992) p. 209.

71. Sudbury Valley may be the only school in the world where the cost per student has risen only at the rate of inflation over a period of four decades!

72. For an example of such reexamination, see Daniel Greenberg, *A Clearer View* (Framingham, MA: Sudbury Valley School Press, 2000).

73. *Kingdom of Childhood* (Framingham, MA: Sudbury Valley School Press, 1994) is a collection of three dozen retrospectives of life at school, provided by former students who spanned a wide range of interests and character types.

74. *Ibid.,* Chapter 1.

75. *Legacy of Trust* (Framingham, MA: Sudbury Valley School Press, 1992) and *Pursuit of Happiness* (Framingham, MA: Sudbury Valley School Press, 2005). The former book contains in two appendices two earlier studies.

76. *Pursuit of Happiness* (Framingham, MA: Sudbury Valley School Press, 2005) pp. 232, 334, 335.

Index

C

free spirit of children. *See* creativity; curiosity

funding
- ease in locating, 84, 88
- for ideal schools, 153-158

G

Galileo, 45

global mind, 58

graduate education, ideal characteristics of, 139-145

graduation from Sudbury Valley School, 166-167

Greek philosophers, effect on modern science, 81

Greenberg, Michael, 107

growth, development versus, xix

H

health-care system example (obtaining wisdom), 19-20

Henry, Jules, 29

Heraclitus, 86

hierarchical social structures, individual realization in, 92

Highet, Gilbert, 56

history of liberal democracy, 93

human beings, educational tools natural to, 99-105

human nature
- communication as part of, 107, 113
- conflict with industrial culture, 55
- curiosity as part of, 113-114
- decoration as part of, 107, 113
- music as part of, 107, 113
- play as part of, 113-114

humanities, relationship with science, 44-46

I

ideal schools, funding for, 153-158

idealized redesign, 121-123

ideals of United States, 65-69

ideas
- dissemination, ease in, 84
- exchanging, ease in, 83, 88
- feedback, ease of, 84, 88

imagination in modern science, 81-82

immersion as education in liberal democracy, 94-98

inalienable rights. *See* individual rights

independence, learning, 130

India, computer literacy experiment, 15-16

Indian birthrate example, 87

individual realization
- in developed society, 79-89
- in hierarchical social structures, 92
- in liberal democracy, 91-98
- obstructions to, 87-89

individual rights, 65-66
- in liberal democracy, 93
- in schools, lack of, 67

industrialization. *See also* post-industrial era
  core elements of, 82
  development of mass schooling, xvii-xviii
  effect on educational aspects, xx-xxi
industrialized nature of schools, 49-56
infants
  communication with, 129-130
  learning in, 125-131
information, definition of, 18
inner-city literacy example, 10-14
instruction, definition of, 9
internal motivation for learning, 10-14
interpersonal communication. *See* communication; language
intrinsic functions of education, xix

J–K

job security in education system, 71-73
jokes, as creativity example, 36

K-12 schools, ideal characteristics of, 135-138
knowledge
  accessibility of, 83, 88
  definition of, 18
  rate of change, 46-48
  as result of analysis, 61
Kozol, Jonathan, 54
Kulkarni, Manu, 108

L

Laing, Ronald D., 29
language. *See also* communication
  purpose of, 92, 95
  role in education, 103-104
  standardization of, 95
leaders, defined, 116
leadership
  as an art, 114-117
  nurturing ability for, 117
  requirements for, 115-116
learning. *See also* education; schooling
  classes of content of, 18
  collaborative learning with computers, 17
  continuing education and, 147-150
  in infants, 125-131
  interconnectedness with work and play, 46-48
  in K-12 schools, ideal characteristics of, 135-138
  for learning's sake, 147-150
  methods of, 4-5
  from mistakes, 74-75
  motivation for, 10-14
  play, necessity of, 47-48
  in preschool children, 125-134
  during "retirement," 151-152
  role of explanation in, 5-7
  teaching versus, 3-10
  wisdom, obtaining, 18-22
legitimate desires, xix
liberal democracy, individual realization in, 91-98

practices, learning in graduate education, 141-142

Prasad, Devi, 109

preschool children, learning in, 125-134

private schools, financing operating expenses and capital expenses, 155

problem solving, 27-31
definition of, 32
in failing schools, 35
role in education, 102
separating solutions by discipline, 39-44

problems
definition of, 27
methods of treating, 31-35
in practices, 141

prospective explanations, 19

protecting children from danger, 130

public education. See mass schooling

public schools, financing operating expenses and capital expenses, 155

puzzles, as creativity example, 36

Q-R

questions, definition of, 28

rate of accomplishment, 85

rate of change of knowledge, 46-48

rational thought, 81, 87

reading (inner-city example), 10-14

recreative function of art, 114

redesign. See dissolution (of problems)

research cells in graduate education, 142

resistance to change, 71-75

resolution (of problems)
definition of, 31-32
in failing schools, 34

responsibility at Sudbury Valley School, 170

"retirement," learning during, 151-152

retrospective explanations, 19

rights, individual, 65-66
in liberal democracy, 93

role modeling for preschool children, 133

root ideas in American life, 65-69

S

Sadofsky, Mimsy, 161

schooling. See also education; learning
mass schooling
development of, xvii-xviii
industrialized nature of, 49-56
meaning of "teaching" in, 8-9
problem-solving in, 30

schools
building design, 57-58
colleges and universities, ideal characteristics of, 139-145